STUFF

The Secret Lives of Everyday Things

John C. Ryan
Alan Thein Durning

With research assistance by
Sara Jo Breslow
Christy Halvorson
Ankur Tohan

Illustrated by
Don Baker

January 1997

Sightline Institute
Seattle, Washington

Sightline Institute thanks editor and typesetter Ellen W. Chu and reviewers Rey Abruzzi, Jim Cooperman, Bill McKibben, Sandra Postel, Robert Rice, Dave Salman, Betsy Taylor, and John Young for their skilled contributions. We also thank interns Sean Bowles, Rachel Gussett, and Paige Pluymers and volunteers Peter Carlin, Aaron Contorer, Sandra Blair Hernshaw, Norman Kunkel, Flo Lipton, Lyn McCollum, Holly Pearson, Ellen Pyle, Marilyn Roy, Sandra Singler, Scott Stevens, and Lorri Verzola for their dedicated assistance.

Financial support for this book was provided by the Nathan Cummings Foundation, the John D. and Catherine T. MacArthur Foundation, and contributors to Sightline Institute. These include hundreds of individuals and the Bullitt Foundation, C. S. Fund, Ford Foundation, Global Environment Project Institute, William and Flora Hewlett Foundation, Henry P. Kendall Foundation, Merck Family Fund, Surdna Foundation, Turner Foundation, Weeden Foundation, and an anonymous Canadian foundation. Views expressed are the authors' and do not necessarily represent those of Sightline Institute or its directors, officers, staff, or funders. Sightline Institute is a 501(c)(3) tax-exempt organization governed by a board of directors comprising Lester R. Brown of Washington, D.C.; Sandi Chamberlain of Victoria, B.C.; Alan Thein Durning of Seattle; Jane Lubchenco of Corvallis, Ore.; Tyree Scott of Seattle; and Rosita Worl of Juneau.

This book was printed in Vancouver, B.C., using soybean-based ink and recycled paper. Text: 100 percent postconsumer waste. Cover: 100 percent postconsumer waste. Design by Visible Images, Seattle.

Excerpts from this report may be printed in periodicals with written permission from Sightline Institute.

1402 Third Avenue, Suite 500
Seattle, WA 98101-2130
Tel: (206)447-1880; fax: (206)447-2270
e-mail: askus@sightline.org
Web: www.sightline.org

TABLE OF CONTENTS

PROLOGUE

120 POUNDS

My name is Dana, and I...am a consumer. Today, as soon as I got out of bed, I started consuming. I had a coffee. I ate breakfast. I read a newspaper. I put on my clothes. I commuted to work. All day long I went about my ordinary business, consuming stuff and unwittingly affecting places and people around the world.

This book follows a day in the life of a fictional, typical North American—a middle-class resident of Seattle. It is a day in which nothing terribly unusual or dramatic happens. Or so it seems.

I don't usually think of myself as a consumer. Though I don't spend much time worrying about the environment, I don't have a wasteful lifestyle either. I recycle. I have a compost bin in my garden. I've even biked to work before.

North Americans have grown more concerned and knowledgeable about the environment in recent years. And many environmental problems—urban smog, water pollution, lead in our air—are less pronounced than they were just a couple of decades ago.

But cleaning out my basement recently got me thinking. Though it felt good to throw out all that junk, my back was sore for a week afterward. Wading through all the objects of my life was a chore. Making them in the first place must have been one too.

Americans throw out about four pounds of garbage each in their daily trash. It's not much in the grand scheme of things. Though they see only a fraction of it, Americans consume 120 pounds—

nearly their average body weight—every day in natural resources extracted from farms, forests, rangelands, and mines.

There I was, piling old paint cans into a cardboard box when something caught my eye. It was a sticker that had fallen off the back of who-knows-what stowed in the basement. It said, "Made in Taiwan." I'd seen thousands of such stickers in my life without ever giving them a second thought. Taiwan. Taiwan. Not just a word on a sticker. It's an island. A country. A real place with real people across an ocean from me.

Suddenly, the overloaded shelves around me looked different. I was stripped of the illusion that stuff comes from stores and is carted "away" by garbage trucks: everything on those shelves came from a real place on the Earth and will go to some other place when I'm done with it. Everything had a history—a trail of causes and effects—and a future. Everything had a life, of sorts. If you tried very hard, you could put a "Made in _____" sticker on each car wax bottle, speaker component, or old magazine on those shelves.

Consumption on the North American scale—our own body weight each day—is possible only because of chains of production that reach all over the planet. Most of the production, and most of its impacts, are hidden from view—in rural hinterlands, fenced-off industrial sites, and far-off nations.

I started wondering where the things in my life come from. As coffee beans, newspapers, and soda

Per Capita Resource Consumption in the United States, Mid-1990s

Material	Pounds Per Day
Stone and cement	27
Coal	19
Miscellaneous minerals	17
Oil	16
Farm products	12
Wood	11
Range grass	10
Metals	8
Natural gas	1
Total	**121**

cans make their ways toward me, what wakes do they leave behind, rippling outward across the world? And what had to happen
for millions of people like me to go about our ordinary business,
using lots of stuff?

*What happens around the world to support a day in the life of a
North American is surprising, dramatic, even disturbing. Multiplied
by the billion members of the world's consumer societies, it adds up
to stresses greater than the world can withstand.*

*It does not have to be this way. A quiet revolution in our way of
life—different technologies, more balanced lifestyles, greener infra-
structure, and better laws—could give us a future where ordinary
life in prosperous societies has only innocuous impacts. Ushering in
these changes can seem impossible. It is not. Just like a jigsaw puzzle,
all the needed pieces are already there. But it takes some effort to
get them into place.*

The first step toward solving any problem is recognizing it. I've
started by looking at the things in my life in a new way and learning what I can about their secret lives.

⚠ Warning to Readers

Consuming too much *Stuff* at one time can be bad for you. Reviewers of
early drafts reported feeling overwhelmed or depressed after learning
the true stories of how things are made. We did, too, when we tried to
read the book straight through. So we lightened the text: editing out
technical details and highlighting alternatives, fun trivia, and even a joke
or two. But *Stuff* still has an emotional punch: the impacts of our
economy on the world *are* disturbing. Pace yourself; skip ahead if you
need to. Expect to be informed, hope to be inspired, but prepare to be
unpleasantly surprised.

COFFEE

The buzzing would not go away. Without opening my eyes, I hit the clock radio. My brain managed to hold one coherent thought: caffeine.

Beans I staggered into the kitchen to brew a cup of coffee. It took 100 beans—about one-sixtieth of the beans that grew on the coffee tree that year. The tree was on a small mountain farm in the Antioquia region of Colombia. The region was cleared of most of its native cloud forests at the turn of the century: the fertile valley bottoms by cattle ranchers and the less productive hillsides by poor farmers who planted coffee and fruit trees. Colombia's forests make it a biological superpower: though the country covers less than 1 percent of the Earth's land surface, it is home to 18 percent of the world's plant species and more types of birds than any other nation.

Dense, manicured rows of *Coffea arabica* trees covered the farm, growing under the strong tropical sun. For most of this century, coffee grew on this farm in the shade of taller fruit and hardwood trees, whose canopies harbored numerous birds, from keel-billed toucans to Canada warblers. In the 1980s, farm owners sawed down most of the shade trees and planted high-yielding varieties of coffee. This change increased their harvests. It also increased soil erosion and decimated birds, including wintering songbirds that breed near my home. Biologists report finding just 5 percent as many bird species in these new, sunny coffee fields as in the traditional shaded coffee plantations they replaced.

With the habitats of birds and other insect eaters removed, pests proliferated and coffee growers stepped up their pesticide

Gulp!

I drink two cups a day. At that rate, I'll down 34 gallons of java this year, made from 18 pounds of beans. Colombian farms have 12 coffee trees growing to support my personal addiction. Farmers will apply 11 pounds of fertilizers and a few ounces of pesticides to the trees this year. And Colombia's rivers will swell with 43 pounds of coffee pulp stripped from my beans.

Coffee is the world's second largest legal export commodity (after oil) and is the second largest source of foreign exchange for developing nations. The United States drinks about one-fifth of the world's coffee.

use. Farmworkers wearing shorts, T-shirts, and sloshing backpacks sprayed my tree with several doses of pesticides synthesized in Germany's Rhine River Valley. Some of the chemicals entered the farmworkers' lungs; others washed or wafted away, only to be absorbed by plants and animals.

Workers earning less than a dollar a day picked my coffee berries by hand and fed them into a diesel-powered crusher, which removed the beans from the pulpy berries that encased them. The pulp was dumped into the Cauca River. The beans, dried under the sun, traveled to New Orleans on a ship in a 132-pound bag. For each pound of beans, about two pounds of pulp had been dumped into the river. As the pulp decomposed, it consumed oxygen needed by fish in the river.

The freighter that carried my coffee was made in Japan and fueled by Venezuelan oil. The shipyard built the freighter out of Korean steel. The Korean steel mill used iron mined on aboriginal lands in the Hamersley Range of western Australia.

The Coffee Tree

The tree, like most Western Hemisphere coffee, was descended from a Javanese seedling brought to the Caribbean in 1721. This seedling in turn descended from *Coffea* shrubs in the forests of Ethiopia. In 1970, windborne spores of African coffee rust landed in Brazil and began to spread north, triggering panic in the Latin American coffee industry.

Breeders went to the dwindling forests of southwestern Ethiopia—coffee's evolutionary home—and found wild varieties resistant to 27 of 33 known types of *la roya* ("the rust"). They returned to South America and crossbred commercial and wild strains.

Governments also reacted to *la roya* by "technifying" coffee farms—removing shade trees, introducing new varieties, and boosting chemical use. Ironically, *la roya* has not spread as feared, probably because the cool temperatures and the dry season in most Latin American highlands limit its growth.

At New Orleans, the beans were roasted for 13 minutes at 400 °F. The roaster burned natural gas pumped from the ground in Texas. The beans were packaged in four-layer bags constructed of polyethylene, nylon, aluminum foil, and polyester. They were trucked to a Seattle warehouse in an 18-wheeler, which got six miles per gallon of diesel. A smaller truck then took the roasted beans to my neighborhood grocery store.

Bag I carried the beans out of the store in a sealed, wax-lined paper bag and a large brown paper sack, both made at unbleached kraft paper mills in Oregon. (Sometimes I bring my own canvas grocery bag, but this time I forgot.) I brought them home in my car; it burned one-fifth of a gallon of gasoline during the five-mile round-trip to the market.

Grinder In the kitchen, I measured the beans in a disposable plastic scoop molded in New Jersey and spooned them into a grinder. The grinder was assembled in China from imported steel, aluminum, copper, and plastic parts. It was powered by electricity generated at Ross Dam on the Skagit River in the Washington Cascades.

I dumped the ground coffee in a gold-plated mesh filter made in Switzerland of German steel and Russian gold. I put the filter into a plastic-and-steel drip coffeemaker.

Water I poured eight ounces of tap water into the appliance. The water came by pipe from a processing plant. Originally it came from the Chester Morse Reservoir on the Cedar River on the west slope of the Cascades. An element heated the water to more than 200 °F. The hot water seeped through the ground coffee and dissolved some of its oils and solids. The brew trickled into a glass carafe; I poured it into a mug with a "Made in Taiwan" sticker hidden underneath. Later, I washed the mug, using much more water than I drank from it.

Sugar I measured out two teaspoons of sugar. It came from cane fields—former sawgrass marshes—south of Lake Okeechobee in Florida. Water that used to flow across these marshes and into the Everglades is now drained into canals and sent directly to the ocean. Or else it irrigates the fields, where it picks up nutrients and pesticides. Populations of all vertebrates—from turtles to storks—have fallen 75 to 95 percent in Everglades National Park. In November 1996, Florida voters rejected a plan to tax sugar growers to help pay for efforts to restore the Everglades.

Cream I stirred in one ounce of cream. The cream came from a grain-fed dairy cow in the Skagit Valley north of Seattle. The cow liked to wade into a stream to drink and to graze on streamside grasses and willows. As a result, the water got warmer and muddier, making life difficult for the coho salmon and steelhead trout living in the stream.

Wastes The cow's manure was rich in nitrogen and phosphorus. The soils of the cow pasture were unable to absorb all the manure, so it washed into the stream when it rained. The infusion of nutrients fertilized algae; decaying manure and algae absorbed oxygen from the water, making life still more difficult for fish.

Two hours after I finished my morning cup, my body had metabolized the coffee. Most of the water and some nutrients passed into the Seattle sewer system. They were carried by Cedar River water and mixed with other organic and inorganic wastes. They traveled under the streets of the city to Seattle's West Point sewage treatment plant on the shores of Puget Sound, next to Discovery Park.

There the solids were filtered, concentrated, digested, and sterilized with screens, settling tanks, bacteria, and chlorine. An engineer deemed the sewage sludge clean enough for agriculture, and a trucker hauled it to pulpwood tree farms for use as fertilizer and soil conditioner. An underwater pipe carried the treated liquids a mile into Puget Sound. The flushing of the tides would eventually carry the liquids into the Pacific Ocean.

What to Do?!

- Find some shade. Coffee grown under the shade of mixed trees requires few or no chemical inputs: the leaf litter replenishes soil nutrients, and the variety of tree species benefits birds and discourages pest outbreaks. Many brands of shade coffee—often labeled as organic or cooperatively produced—are available.
- Go local. Organic mint tea is grown in Oregon's Willamette Valley with no chemical inputs and requires much less energy to be processed and transported (200 miles to Seattle) than coffee. Besides, caffeine makes you jumpy, coffee stains your teeth, and who likes coffee breath anyway?

NEWSPAPER

I put down my coffee to find the morning paper somewhere in my front yard. It was in the bushes again. I pulled the paper out of the plastic bag and the rubber band it came in.

The paper was a half pound (220 grams) of newsprint covered with two grams of petroleum- and soybean-based inks. Two-thirds of the pages, and two-thirds of the ink, were devoted to advertising. I mostly read the comics. Two-thirds of American adults read a newspaper on an average weekday; three-fourths do on a Sunday.

Trees The paper was half recycled and half made from trees. Most of the trees (those that provided 45 percent of the newsprint) were 150-year-old Engelmann spruce and subalpine fir trees in the Cariboo Mountains of central British Columbia. Canada is the world's leading newsprint producer; B.C. alone produces 5 percent of the world total. Loggers, earning Can$20 (US$15) an hour and wielding Husqvarna chainsaws, felled the trees from a steep slope above Penfold Creek. They were lucky to have jobs: many of their friends were laid off in the 1980s as machines did more of the cutting and processing of trees. From 1980 to 1990, the number of timber industry jobs in B.C. fell by a third even as the volume of wood cut in the province increased 16 percent.

Except for a 160-foot-wide strip of selective logging along the creek, loggers and their machines removed every tree for 100 acres. Clearcutting of wildlands accounts for 90 percent of logging in British Columbia. Some clearcuts in the Cariboo Mountains are so large they can be seen from space. (I took a rafting trip in B.C. last summer and heard a joke about the local definition of selective logging: select a mountain, then log it!)

Logging Roads After the branches and treetops were sawed off, a choker-setter in a hard hat attached cables to the trees, and a diesel-powered yarder dragged them up the hillside to a muddy landing area, leaving a "skid trail" on the slope. Mud and rocks tumbled toward the creek. The logs were loaded on an 18-wheel flatbed truck. The driver found his way through a dozen gears and steered his load over dirt logging roads that twisted and turned through the mountains like so much spaghetti. He made his way to a sawmill in Quesnel, a town beside the Fraser River. The Fraser is the world's greatest producer of salmon, but logging, road building, and other disturbance of the watershed have contributed to an 80 percent decline in salmon over the past century.

With the next rain, more mud and rocks spilled from the road and the skid trails into Penfold Creek, smothering sockeye salmon eggs in the gravel bed of the stream. British Columbia has roughly 150,000 miles of logging roads—enough to circle the planet six times. The B.C. Ministry of Forests plans to remove 3,000 miles annually to reduce the damage to fish and wildlife. It also plans to build twice as many miles of new logging roads each year.

Pulp The Quesnel mill sawed the logs. About half of each log was converted into lumber; the rest became chips and sawdust. These residues were trucked to a nearby pulp mill, where they were mixed with Fraser River water and cooked to make a pulp of weak, yellow fibers. Hydroelectricity from a dam on the Peace River (which runs from northeastern B.C. toward the Arctic Ocean) powered both mills. This "mechanical pulping" managed to convert 95 percent of the wood residues into pulp. It made a low-grade pulp that would quickly yellow with age or exposure to sunlight. The pulp was lightly bleached with hydrogen peroxide.

Five percent of the newsprint in my morning paper came from another forest and was processed in a "kraft" pulp mill in Crofton, on British Columbia's Vancouver Island. Newsprint makers add kraft pulp to mechanical pulp to make their product stronger. (*Kraft* is German for strength; kraft pulping yields longer and stronger fibers than other pulping processes.) The kraft pulp began as 300-year-old western red cedar and hemlock trees. They were logged in a temperate rain forest in the Paradise watershed on the mainland coast of British Columbia. (I've always wanted to see this coast by taking the ferry up the Inside Passage to Alaska. I guess I should go soon, before much more of it is clearcut.)

Trucks carried the logs over a muddy logging road to the shore. A tugboat hauled them to a sawmill on Vancouver Island, and the resulting chips and dust were trucked to Crofton. Then the chips cooked in a soup of caustic soda and sodium sulfide. These chemicals are not especially toxic, but they combine to give Crofton the rotten-egg aroma of a mill town.

After nearly 12 hours in a giant cooker, the tightly bound wood fibers had separated from one another. The pulp was then washed to remove undigested knots of wood and chemicals (for reuse). The mill converted about 50 percent of the incoming wood to pulp; the rest it burned for energy.

Bleaching   The kraft pulp—brown like a paper grocery bag— was then bleached with chlorine dioxide. A tiny fraction of the chlorine reacted with organic chemicals in the pulp to form various dioxins and furans, among them TCDD and TCDF—two of the most carcinogenic substances known. Beyond causing cancer, dioxins can also suppress the immune system and produce severe birth defects and reproductive disorders in humans and other animals. Pulp mills in B.C. have dramatically reduced their toxic emissions since the late 1980s; average discharges of TCDD dropped by 85 percent from 1990 to 1993.

Your Choices Matter

European consumers' demands for totally chlorine-free (TCF) paper, along with increasingly strict regulations in Canada on mill emissions, have led many mills to switch partially to making TCF pulp. Canada's export-oriented paper industry is extremely sensitive to shifting tastes in foreign markets. Some mills simultaneously produce chlorine-free paper for the European market and chlorine-bleached paper for the U.S. market.

Similarly, California's legislation requiring newsprint to have at least 35 percent recycled content by 1996 and 50 percent by the year 2000 has sent paper mills in the U.S. and Canada scurrying to boost their recycling capacity.

Pulping the virgin fibers in Crofton and Quesnel required nearly a third of a kilowatt-hour of energy, enough to power the refrigerator in my kitchen for two hours. Some of the energy came from wood waste burned at the mills. Burning the wood generated heat and smoke and released carbon dioxide, the principal climate-altering greenhouse gas. The seedlings planted in the Paradise clearcut will absorb carbon dioxide as they grow. But these seedlings are to be logged again in 60 years—long before they can recapture the CO_2 emitted in turning 300-year-old trees into newsprint. Logging of coastal rain forests is responsible for one-fourth of British Columbia's greenhouse gas emissions.

Overall, virgin newsprint (which is mostly mechanical pulp) has lower environmental impacts than most virgin paper: making mechanical pulp requires less energy and water and fewer chemical additives than making kraft pulp. Mechanical pulp is not chlorine bleached. It is also easier to de-ink and recycle than other papers. That is why curbside recycling programs, including the one in my neighborhood, collect newsprint separately.

Recycling From the mills in Quesnel and Crofton, the pulp was trucked to a paper mill in Spokane, Washington. Canada provides more than half the virgin pulp in U.S. newsprint. The paper

Reduce, Reuse, Reboot

Collecting paper waste and turning it into a quarter pound of recycled newsprint for my morning paper took approximately half as much energy and water as did logging and transporting trees and turning them into a quarter pound of virgin paper. It also caused less air and water pollution. Yet even recycling is an energy hog compared to paperless publishing. With the energy used to make my newspaper, I could have browsed online newspapers on my computer for at least six hours.

mill combined the virgin pulp with recycled pulp—80 percent old newspapers and 20 percent old magazines. A truck had collected the papers curbside at homes in Spokane; the magazines were unsold copies returned from newsstands. Magazine publishers routinely print far more magazines than they sell; most go to landfills.

To make the recycled pulp, blades churned old papers and magazines together in a tank of warm water and detergent. Clay fillers from the magazine paper and the detergent combined to clean the ink off the paper. The ink adhered to air bubbles in the tank and rose to the surface, where machinery skimmed it off like cream. Most of the waste paper turned back to pulp, but 15 percent of it (including both fibers and ink) became sludge, which truckers hauled to a landfill. Because the recycling process weakens paper fibers, newsprint can be recycled only three or four times; it is then replaced with virgin fibers.

Printing   The mill in Spokane formed the paper and spun it into massive rolls, each four and a half feet wide and four feet across and weighing about a ton. An 18-wheeler hauled the rolls across the Cascades to a printing plant near downtown Seattle. High-speed presses printed the day's edition with black and color inks. The black ink was a mixture of petroleum-based resins and oils from California and a small amount of carbon black made from oil drilled in the Gulf of Mexico. The colored inks were about one-third soybean oil from Illinois, with small amounts of petrochemical pigments added. The inks were produced in Kent and Tukwila, industrial suburbs south of Seattle.

The newspaper came to my neighborhood in a gasoline-fueled station wagon. The driver lobbed the paper toward my front door but hit the bushes instead. The paper was bound in a rubber band (made in Hong Kong from petroleum) and wrapped in a clear sheath of low-density polyethylene plastic from New Jersey. I saved the rubber band and threw out the bag.

I scanned the front section, read "Dilbert" and a few other comics, and dropped the paper in my recycling bin. It was one of 38 million newspapers recycled daily in the United States; 22 million others are thrown away each day. Later, a diesel recycling truck hauled the paper to a warehouse. Depending on fluctuating market prices, my paper would either become newsprint again, go into cardboard, or be exported to Asia.

What to Do?!

- Share a subscription with a friend. Have your paper and halve your impact.
- Share a subscription with dozens of strangers: read the newspaper at a library.
- Don't subscribe if you don't read the paper every day. Buy papers when you're actually going to read them.
- Lobby your paper to maximize its recycled content and use no pulp from old growth forests.
- Read alternative news sources, such as *Cascadia Times*, *High Country News*, *In These Times*, or *Washington Free Press*. Bypass the advertising and fluff that fill most newspapers and learn more about your world.

T-SHIRT

I changed out of my pajamas. I put on a T-shirt. Without noticing, I seem to have accumulated an endless number of T-shirts. (I wonder if they mate and reproduce in my laundry pile.)

My T-shirt was half polyester and half cotton and weighed about four ounces.

Polyester The polyester in my shirt started as a few tablespoons of petroleum. By buying the T-shirt, I helped send an oil derrick's spinning diamond drill bit into the ground near Maracaibo, on the Caribbean coast of Venezuela. Sensors near the bit sent data on mile-deep rocks to computers at the surface, which then redirected the bit until it hit pay dirt, drilling all the while. The derrick used "drilling muds" containing diesel fuel, heavy metals, and water to flush away bits of rock and to lubricate and cool the diamond bit. After the drill found the petroleum deposit, pumps brought oil and gas to the surface; drops of crude oil leaked from derricks, pipelines, and storage tanks. Drilling muds, along with a witch's brew of other hydrocarbons, saturated the soils of the field.

Crude oil is composed of many different hydrocarbons and small amounts of impurities. A refinery in Curaçao, in the Netherlands Antilles, washed the oil with water to remove corrosive salts. Then 4 percent of the crude oil was burned to heat the rest to 750°F. The oil was pumped into a 12-story steel tower.

All but the heaviest tars evaporated and rose through the tower. As they rose, they cooled and condensed. The heavier hydrocarbons condensed more quickly and were drawn off; they would be processed into waxes and lubricants (like the oil I use in my car). Lighter compounds rose higher and, after several more rounds of energy-intensive processing, became various grades of fuels and raw materials for petrochemicals like polyester.

Fashioning Polyester

From the oil field to the garment factory gate, making my shirt's polyester released one-fourth the polyester's weight in air pollution, counting nitrogen and sulfur oxides, hydrocarbons, particulates, carbon monoxide, and heavy metals. These pollutants impair breathing, aggravate lung and heart diseases, and suppress the immune system, among other harmful effects.

Making the polyester also released 10 times the polyester's weight in carbon dioxide, helping destabilize the global climate.

Only about 3 percent of the oil refined in the United States is used to make petrochemicals; most oil becomes gasoline and diesel fuel. Oil refining pumps more tons of pollution into the air than any other U.S. industry except steelmaking.

The refinery "cracked" some of the hydrocarbons at high temperatures into lighter, smaller molecules, such as the ethylene and xylene used to make my polyester. A chemical plant near Wilmington, Delaware, turned ethylene into ethylene glycol with the help of heat and heavy-metal catalysts such as cadmium acetate. Catalysts are amazing substances: they hasten chemical reactions without themselves being consumed; theoretically, if none is spilled or lost, a finite amount could be used forever.

Through various high-temperature chemical reactions, the plant converted the xylene to DMT (dimethyl terephthalate). DMT and ethylene glycol were combined and then chemically linked into long chains to form PET (polyethylene terephthalate). PET is one of the most common petrochemicals, found in drink containers, clothing, and other plastic products. The United States produced more than 64 billion pounds of plastics in 1994—more than 250 pounds per person. Almost a third of this became packaging—a fact that doesn't surprise me, considering how much plastic ends up in my trash.

Tiny amounts of catalysts and other toxic compounds escaped from the Wilmington plant. The PET resin was drawn apart until it formed hairlike filaments—polyester fiber.

Cotton My two ounces of cotton came from 14 square feet of cropland in Mississippi. The soil was first fumigated with aldicarb, one of the most toxic pesticides applied in the U.S. Wind carried some of the soil, and some of the aldicarb, into nearby streams. The cotton seed was also dipped in a fungicide. Cotton accounts for 10 percent of the world's annual pesticide consumption.

As the seeds germinated in the soil, a farmworker drove a tractor with a spray rig behind it and doused the field with a soil sterilant to kill off everything that might compete with or eat young cotton plants. It can take five years of rest from pesticides before healthy populations of earthworms return to soils planted with row crops like cotton. Five more times before harvesting, the field was sprayed with pesticides, mostly organophosphates, which damage the central nervous system. Cotton is also among the world's most heavily irrigated crops, in part because water runs quickly off fields where beneficial soil organisms such as earthworms have been exterminated.

To prevent the leaves from staining or leaving flecks in the white cotton bolls, a crop duster sprayed the field with paraquat (a defoliant) just before harvesting. About half the paraquat missed its target and drifted onto nearby fields and streams. Then a worker driving a large cotton stripper with an air-conditioned cab picked the cotton. The cotton stripper was manufactured in the United States using parts imported from more than 20 countries. It burned diesel fuel from Mexico.

A cotton gin separated the fibers from the seeds. The seeds were pressed to make cooking oil and livestock feed. The clean fibers were sent to a textile mill in North Carolina, which carded them, blended them with the polyester fibers, and spun the two into yarn. The yarn was treated with polystyrene to make it easier to handle.

Dyes Another textile mill knitted the cotton-and-polyester yarn into fabric; mineral oil fed continuously into the knitting machine reduced friction. Workers then washed out the oils and bleached, dyed, and finished the fabric with industrial chemicals, including chlorine, chromium, and formaldehyde. Cotton resists coloring; one-third of the dyes did not adhere and were carried off in the wastewater stream. Textile dyes are regulated by the U.S. Environmental Protection Agency (EPA) as hazardous substances.

Sewing My fabric was shipped to Honduras. Honduran women in a Taiwanese-owned apparel factory cut and sewed it into a T-shirt; they earned about 30 cents an hour. They mounted my shirt on a cardboard sheet made of pinewood pulp from Georgia, wrapped it in a polyethylene bag from Mexico, and stacked it in a corrugated box from Maine.

The box went by freighter to Baltimore, by train to San Francisco, and by truck to Seattle. It was unpacked onto a department store shelf under a 150-watt floodlamp. That's where I found it. I bought it because I liked its earth-tone color. I brought it home by car in a bag of low-density polyethylene from Louisiana.

Laundry I spilled coffee on myself and had to change into a fresh shirt. I threw the dirty one down the laundry chute.

Later, I washed it in water heated to 140°F by natural gas flames. Boxed powder detergent and chlorine bleach from a high-density polyethylene bottle removed the coffee from the fabric. My coffee, detergent, and bleach washed into Seattle's sewer system. An electric dryer evaporated the water from my shirt. The washing machine used about twice as much energy as the dryer to run the load of laundry.

The greatest environmental impacts associated with my T-shirt arose in my own laundry room: washing and drying the shirt just

Sun-Dried Ts

Try using a clothesline. Clotheslines need only solar energy and don't wear your clothes out the way a dryer can. Fact: The United States receives more energy in the form of sunlight in 40 minutes than from all the fossil fuels it burns in a year.

once demanded one-tenth as much energy as manufacturing it in the first place. Over its useful lifetime, washing and drying will dwarf the energy that went into making the shirt. Laundering will also generate the vast majority of solid waste in the shirt's life cycle, in the form of sewage sludge and detergent packaging.

I took the shirt out of the dryer and wondered about the designer's oversized logo on the front: shouldn't *they* be paying *me* to wear their advertising?

What to Do?!

- Wash only full loads of laundry. Avoid using hot water: it takes more energy and breaks down fabrics more quickly than colder water. Wash your clothes when they need washing, not necessarily every time you wear them.
- If you need a new washing machine, buy an energy- and water-efficient front-loader rather than a top-loader.
- Heat and cool your body more, your building less. T-shirts in summer save on air conditioning, a far bigger energy hog than clothing. Likewise, extra clothes in winter save on heat.
- Buy and sell at "vintage" (used) clothing stores. Rescue something from the landfill and be retro-trendy at the same time.
- Look for organic cotton products and undyed cotton. Such cotton is becoming more widely available: in 1989, there were 100 acres of organic cotton in the United States; by 1994, there were 18,000.
- Support activist groups working to make agriculture environmentally friendly.

SHOES

I put on my sneakers—"cross-trainers," I guess they're called—and got ready to go to work. I don't "cross-train"; I'm not sure I even know what it is. But I do wear the shoes a lot.

Eighty percent of athletic shoes in the United States are not used for their designed purpose. As an executive for L.A. Gear put it, "If you're talking performance shoes, you need only one or two pair. If you're talking fashion, you're talking endless pairs of shoes." According to surveys, U.S. women own between 15 and 25 pairs of shoes, men 6 to 10 pairs. Americans spend twice as much on children's athletic shoes as they do on children's books.

My two shoes weighed about a pound and were composed of dozens of different, mostly synthetic, materials. Like almost all athletic shoes sold in the United States, they were manufactured overseas by an obscure firm contracting to the company whose name and logo actually appeared on the shoes. Mine were assembled in a Korean-owned factory in Tangerang, an industrial district outside of Jakarta, Indonesia. But almost all the component parts were made elsewhere.

The shoe company in Oregon specified the shoes' high-tech design and materials and relayed the plans by satellite to a computer-aided-design firm in Taiwan. This firm faxed plans to engineers in South Korea.

In the 1980s, South Korea was a leading exporter of athletic shoes, but democratic reforms, labor unrest, and economic development resulted in shoe workers' wages more than doubling in the four years before 1990. Shoe companies moved to cheaper pastures in China and Southeast Asia. Over the next three years,

Industrial Globetrotters

The manufacture of footwear has become such an interrelated global industry that attempting to determine the composition and manufacturing sites of a shoe's components is often like trying to unscramble the proverbial egg. —Journal of Commerce

With modern industries freely roaming the planet, it can be difficult for any single government, labor union, or activist group to have much leverage on corporate behavior. If pushed too hard, a company may relocate—or at least threaten to do so. Ultimately, by voting with their pocketbooks for responsibly made products, consumers have the most influence over the practices of far-flung corporations.

employment in South Korea's shoe industry fell by three-fourths; nearly 400,000 Koreans lost their jobs.

Leather My shoes had three main parts: the logo-covered upper, the shock-absorbing midsole, and the waffle-treaded outsole. The upper had about 20 different parts. It was mostly cow leather. The cow was raised, slaughtered, and skinned in Texas. Most of the carcass became human and pet food. The hide was cured with salt and stacked with 750 others in a 20-foot container and carried by freight train from Amarillo to Los Angeles. From there it was shipped to Pusan, South Korea. Most U.S. hides are exported for tanning: labor costs and environmental standards are lower overseas.

Tanning makes leather soft and keeps it from decaying. For centuries, tanning meant soaking animal hides in tannins from bark and vegetable extracts; today it usually entails a 20-step process with large spinning drums and solutions of chrome, calcium hydroxide, and other strong chemicals. Chrome tanning (including unhairing, deliming, pickling, tanning, retanning, dyeing, and lubricating) can be done in a day; vegetable tanning can take weeks.

Workers in Pusan loaded the tanned leather onto an airplane headed to Jakarta, while the tanning plant discharged hair, epidermis, leather scraps, and processing chemicals into the Naktong River. Much of South Korea's tap water is not fit for human consumption because it is tainted with metals and other pollutants from heavy industry.

Synthetics Except for the leather, my shoes were made from petroleum-based chemicals. The midsole was a custom-designed EVA (ethylene vinyl acetate) foam: a composite of several substances, each with its own valued properties. Ethylene made the mix easy to mold, vinyl made it resilient, and acetate made it strong and stiff. One of the most important building blocks for making synthetic chemicals, ethylene is a colorless, slightly sweet-smelling, yet toxic gas. It was distilled and "cracked" from Saudi petroleum shipped in a tanker to a Korean refinery.

More ethylene was heated with acetic acid (the main ingredient of vinegar) and a palladium catalyst to form vinyl acetate. The acetic acid didn't come from vinegar: it was synthesized from natural gas and carbon monoxide.

The ethylene and vinyl acetate were mixed with pigments, antioxidants, and catalysts; poured into a mold; and baked. During the ensuing reaction, millions of tiny gas bubbles arose to make a foam. The foam gives my shoes that cushy feel and protects my foot from the impact (two to three times my body weight) each time my heel hits the ground when I run.

Below the heel was my shoe's only component manufactured in the United States: a small amber-colored polyurethane bag filled with (marketing notwithstanding) a pressurized gas of secret composition, not air. (I guess "Pressurized-Gas Jordans" just wouldn't sell like "Air Jordans.")

Rubber My shoes' outer soles were made of styrene-butadiene rubber. The rubber was synthesized from Saudi petroleum and local benzene (made from coal) in a factory in Taiwan. The Taiwanese factory got its electricity from one of the island's three nuclear power plants. Though tree farmers in the tropics still grow natural rubber, about two-thirds of the world's rubber is synthetic. The rubber was formed into large sheets and flown to Jakarta.

In the shoe factory, machines cut up the sheets and molded the grooved tread that I see on the bottom of my shoe. Like too much batter in a waffle iron, some of the rubber oozed out the edges. According to Nike, this excess rubber made up the largest volume of solid waste generated by its shoe factories; it used to be sent to landfills. Now it is ground into a powder and put back into the rubber "batter" for the next batch of shoes. Nike reports cutting its rubber waste by 40 percent with this "Regrind" system, saving 5 million pounds of rubber annually.

Assembly The factory in Tangerang manufactured shoes for Adidas, Nike, and Reebok. Mine happened to be Nikes—not terribly different from the others except for the logo and which athlete was paid to endorse them.

Powerful machines used pressure and sharp blades to precisely cut the leather and other tough materials into shoe parts. A Japanese-made embroidery machine speed-sewed the corporate logo on the sides of my shoes.

Though high-tech equipment helps, putting shoes together remains the domain of hand labor. On the assembly line, several hundred young Javanese women with names like Suraya, Tri, and Yuli cut, sewed, and glued my uppers and soles together to make shoes. The air smelled of paint and glue, and the temperature neared 100 °F. Like most of the workers, Suraya wore cheap rubber flip-flops. She would have to pay more than a month's salary to buy the $75 pair of shoes she helped make for me. She earned the Indonesian minimum wage—650 rupiah (about 23 cents) an hour.

Belabored Points

International shoe companies alternately argue that their presence directly benefits Asian workers, or that they cannot much influence how workers are treated in repressive Asian countries or in factories run by separate companies. Or they insist that their factories comply fully with local government regulations—which isn't saying much. As Rahman, a 20-year-old hot-press operator in a Jakarta shoe factory, explained, "We need protection from our government. We don't need foreign companies to come to Indonesia to take advantage of [President] Suharto's denial of human rights."

Under the discotheque-like glow of black lights, Suraya brushed a sparkling, solvent-based glue across the bottom of my midsole to attach it to my rubber outsole. The glue contained luminous dyes: under the black lights, Suraya could easily see if she had spread it evenly across the entire surface for a tight seal. Other workers glued the sole to the upper (using nontoxic water-based glues as well as toxic solvent-based ones), trimmed and polished my shoe, and inserted the laces and insole.

Discipline was strict, sometimes abusive, in the factory, which was run by ex–military men from Korea. But Suraya knew not to complain about the pay or the illegal, compulsory overtime she sometimes worked. She was replaceable—Indonesia has a huge surplus of cheap labor—and speaking out could mean getting fired, or worse. The Indonesian military routinely intervenes in the country's labor disputes through interrogations, threats, and even murder. The Indonesian government believes that even at $2 a day, workers' wages are too high for the country to compete with lower-wage nations like India and Vietnam.

Though solvent fumes caused health problems for some workers, the shoe factory generated little pollution and required little energy compared with the refineries, chemical plants, and tanneries that produced its raw materials.

Shoe Box My shoes were hand stuffed with lightweight tissue paper (made from Sumatran rainforest trees) and put in a shoe box. The box had been made in a "closed-loop" paper mill in New Mexico that recycled all its sludge. Waste steam from a nearby power plant powered the mill. All Nike shoe boxes are made at this mill.

The box was corrugated cardboard that was 100 percent recycled and unbleached. The corrugated box used 10 percent less pulp than one made of solid cardboard. The box was much improved over old designs: tabs and slots, not toxic petrochemical glues, held it together; its outside was printed with inks that contained no heavy metals.

Folded stacks of empty boxes were shipped west across the Pacific from Los Angeles; boxed shoes were shipped east in a super–container ship carrying 5,000 20-foot containers. Each journey took three weeks. Shoes were the third largest cargo shipped to the United States from eastern Asia in 1995, after toys and auto parts.

As I laced up my shoes, I noticed a small tear over my big toe. At this rate, the pair wouldn't last a year. That's much longer than throwaway items like my newspaper, but still, maybe I could find my old needle and stitch up the hole before it grew. Maybe I could make my shoes last longer, walk more softly on the earth, and save 75 bucks, too.

What to Do?!

- Count the pairs of shoes in your closets. How many do you need?
- Buy durable shoes; when they wear out, have them repaired. Repair is to recycling what recycling is to dumping.
- Choose locally made goods over those made far away.
- Buy secondhand shoes or shoes made from recycled materials.
- Support human rights organizations with your time and money.
- Don't worry too much about what you wear. What you drive, eat, and read matter more.

BIKE (AND CAR)

This morning was warm and clear; I decided to bike to work. I strapped on my helmet and rolled off past the car left sitting in the driveway. I've done this before a few times and always felt better for it. But I keep falling back into driving. Maybe it's because my company gives me a free parking space for my car but no place to shower and change after biking.

Energy I live six miles from my office, a good 20-minute workout on my bike. During the ride, I burned 210 calories—about what's in a plate of spaghetti, and less energy than any other form of transport consumes, even walking. If I had walked to work, I would have used 600 calories of energy—and gotten to work late.

If I had driven, I would have burned a quarter gallon of gasoline (from oil drilled on Alaska's North Slope, piped to a tanker in Prince William Sound, then shipped south and refined in Anacortes, Washington). That much gasoline would yield nearly 8,000 calories of energy—fossil fuel energy, not food energy—nearly 40 times the energy burned riding my bike. The main difference is that when I drive alone, 95 percent of the energy goes to moving the 3,200-pound car itself, not its 140-pound cargo. What a waste! On a bike, which weighs about one-fifth as much as I do, almost all the energy supplied by my muscles propels my body forward.

During the year, I will drive my car 11,600 miles—the average for an American—and buy 464 gallons of gasoline. I will also spend one-fourth of my personal income on transportation: 17 percent using my car, 7 percent on freight charges included in prices of things I buy, and 1 percent in taxes for roads. (My daily commute is shorter than most, but I drive a lot on weekend errands. Why do stores have to be scattered all over town? I also like to drive to my favorite mountain biking spots.)

Pollution On my bike I caused no air pollution (unless you consider sweat air pollution) and made no con-

Let's See What This Baby's Made Of
Composition of a typical 1995 car

Material	Pounds	Percent
Steel	1,767	55
Iron	398	12
Plastics	246	8
Fluids and lubricants	190	6
Aluminum	188	6
Rubber	136	4
Glass	92	3
Copper and brass	44	1
Other metals	49	2
Other materials	98	3
Total	**3,208**	**100**

tribution to global warming. I consumed no oil, gasoline, or other fossil fuels, and sent no toxic chemicals into the air. When I drive to work, my car pumps out nearly five pounds of climate-threatening carbon dioxide, half a pound of health-threatening carbon monoxide, and a few grams each of smog-forming hydrocarbons and nitrogen oxides.

Fossil fuels such as gasoline are the main source of climate-altering CO_2 emissions. In the United States, motor vehicles outnumber registered drivers, and Americans drive as many miles each year as all drivers in the rest of the world combined. Traffic accidents kill more Americans each year than guns or illegal drugs, and they are the leading cause of death for Americans 2 to 24 years old. Car exhaust also kills thousands of Americans annually.

Though my car has a catalytic converter to turn pollutants into CO_2 and water, it doesn't work well on such a short trip, when the engine runs cold. Half of all car trips in the United States are five miles or less—perfect for biking.

Pavement The pavement I rode on was 12-inch-thick asphalt made from Texas petroleum poured over a graded roadbed covered with locally crushed rock. During Seattle's frequent rains, oil,

King of the Road   III·III

High-mileage cars use less energy and pollute less than gas guzzlers. But the only way to tackle all the environmental problems of cars—from energy and material consumption to traffic jams, sprawl, and accidents—is to drive less. Bus, carpool, walk, or, best of all, bike.

A human on a bike moves more efficiently than anything else nature or humans have ever devised. Pound for pound, I use less energy biking a mile than any animal or machine covering the same distance. Even a salmon uses more than twice as much energy per pound to swim a mile!

road salt, and herbicides run off the pavement into Puget Sound. Nearly half of all cars on U.S. highways drip some hazardous fluid. About half the 20 quarts of oil my car used this year either was burned off by the car's engine or found its way onto the ground and into sewers and streams. (I can see the sheen of oil and anti-freeze on my driveway.)

My bike took up a small fraction of the space my car takes on the roads and less than one-twentieth the area for parking. Bike lanes can move two to six times as many people per hour as the same area of pavement devoted to cars. Washington and Oregon already have more miles of roads than they do streams.

Steel My bike weighs 30 pounds—mostly steel, aluminum, rubber, and plastics. The steel in my frame consists of iron with small amounts of carbon, chrome, and molybdenum added to make it harder. Such alloy steels are made in mini-mills that melt down scrap metal.

The 15 pounds of steel in my bike frame, wheels, and other parts began in a Chicago junkyard not far from the mini-mill. The scrap was sorted with magnets and delivered to the mill, where it was melted down in an electric-arc furnace. Three electrodes sent bolts of coal-fired electricity through the metal, and the intense heat melted the scrap. Impurities in my 15 pounds of scrap formed small amounts of gases, two ounces of toxic-laden dust, and a float-ing layer of waste called slag. Removing the waste generated a few grams of sludge tainted with heavy metals. Making steel from scrap uses one-fourth the energy of making steel from iron ore.

Iron Ore Of the 1,800 pounds of steel in my car, 800 pounds began as scrap. Melting the scrap in an electric-arc furnace gener-ated 8 pounds of toxic dust. The other 1,000 pounds of steel and the 400 pounds of iron in my car came from a far dirtier process.

It started with 3,500 pounds of iron ore in an open-pit mine—a giant red crater amid the spruce and pine forests of northern Minnesota. The ore was mined with gigantic Japanese-made machinery, crushed, ground, separated with magnets, and mixed with clay to form pellets. The 2,100 pounds of waste rock, or tailings, was dumped in a large pile near the mine. A barge carried the ore to Gary, Indiana, a steel town on the shores of Lake Michigan.

In a cavernous Gary steel mill, a blast furnace heated the ore with coke from West Virginia and limestone from Indiana to form pure molten iron. Impurities in the ore flowed off as iron-rich slag, which was later recycled into the blast furnace. Burning the coke also generated both carbon monoxide and carbon dioxide. The U.S. steel industry emits twice as much carbon monoxide as the pulp and paper industry, the next largest industrial source. (The largest source is not an industry; it's car exhaust.)

The molten iron was carried in specially lined railcars to the steelmaking furnace, where it was mixed with scrap steel from a salvage yard. Pure oxygen, blasted into the mix at supersonic speeds, kicked off a chemical reaction that melted the scrap and removed

Coke: The Real Thing

The coke was pure carbon made by heating coal to 2000 °F in an oxygen-free oven, then quenching it in water. Coke making is the most polluting stage of steel manufacturing. The quench water picked up volatile organic compounds and suspected carcinogens; it is regulated as toxic waste. The coke oven generated dust and gas containing fine coke particles, sulfur compounds, and an array of toxic chemicals. Some of this toxic gas was captured for reuse; some escaped up the oven's smokestacks. According to the EPA's Toxic Release Inventory, U.S. steelmakers generated 650,000 tons of hazardous waste in 1993, more than any other industry. The mining industry probably generates more but does not have to report its toxic releases to the EPA.

most impurities as slag. Forty-five minutes later, the iron and other inputs had been converted to steel—and to superheated clouds of zinc, lead, and iron oxide dust and more carbon monoxide. Water cooled this exhaust enough for smokestack scrubbers to remove some of the pollutants; these would be reused or trucked to landfills.

Your basic blast furnace reaction:
$$Fe_2O_3 + 3CO \rightarrow 2Fe + 3CO_2$$
Your basic greenhouse gas

Overall, the mill used 31 gallons—250 pounds—of water to make each pound of steel in my car.

All that steel makes my car heavy and strong. One reason I don't bike very often is that it's intimidating to face all those 3,000-pound steel boxes when my only protective gear is a one-pound helmet. But biking is actually safer per mile than driving, especially where there are good bike routes. Besides, if we all try to protect ourselves individually rather than collectively, we'll end up driving army tanks.

Paint   Once the steel for my bike had been molded into tubes, a truck took them to a bicycle factory in Wisconsin, where metal workers cut and welded them into a bike frame. Other workers sanded the frame, cleaned it with chemicals, oven-dried it, and sprayed on powdered paint (made of plastic resins and pigments in Ohio). The oversprayed powder fell through a grate in the floor and was collected for reuse. My bike frame was then baked to melt the paint into a uniform coat. Unlike liquid paint, powdered coatings contain no solvents, so they emit almost no air-polluting volatile organic compounds (VOCs) when sprayed; they also use less energy in baking. VOCs react with sunlight to form smog. Some liquid paint solvents also damage the kidneys and central nervous system and cause asthma, confusion, and fatigue.

My car's body was painted in a Detroit assembly plant. The body was dipped in detergent and a phosphate bath to remove surface debris, then in zinc phosphate and chromic acid to prevent corrosion and help the primer adhere to the metal. The body was submerged in a primer bath and baked, emitting VOCs.

Robots and workers then sprayed six more coats on my car: a sealant (consisting of polyvinyl chloride [PVC] and solvents), an anti-chip layer, a primer, a color coat, a clear coat, and a noise-reducing tar. The oversprayed liquids formed unusable sludges that were trucked to a landfill. Four times in seven coats, the body was baked, causing toxic VOCs to evaporate into the air. Painting is the most polluting process in the automobile assembly plant; the color coat emits the most air pollution.

Assembly Once my bike frame was painted, it went to the assembly line where its various components were installed, mostly by hand. The frame, fork, and wheels were built in the Wisconsin plant; the rest were manufactured elsewhere, mostly in Japan.

The car assembly plant was a giant facility—as big as six football fields—housing a tremendously complex operation. At one end, robots started welding pieces of sheet metal; several hours and miles later, my completed car emerged. Welded in 4,000 spots, it had nearly 10,000 parts manufactured into about 100 major components by companies throughout the world. In all, making my car and its components consumed nearly 40,000 gallons of water, weighing nearly 100 times the car itself. My car's full life story could easily fill a book of its own.

Though making a car is energy intensive and polluting, most of my car's environmental impact comes when I sit behind the wheel. For example, making the car took roughly an eighth as much energy as the car will use during its nine-year lifetime. So my daily decisions about where to go and how to get there matter a lot. And my decisions about where to live matter even more. I know I've been driving less since I moved from the suburbs into Seattle.

Aluminum My bike's eight pounds of aluminum were cast into gears, brakes, spokes, and other parts by a Japanese manufacturer. Smelters in Siberia made the metal from 40 pounds of Australian bauxite ore and hydroelectricity from a dam on Russia's Angara River, the outlet for Lake Baikal. The river was dammed to power aluminum smelters. The surface of the lake—the world's largest—rose three feet, flooding wetlands and island habitats of the nerpa, the world's only freshwater seal. The inefficient smelters have also severely polluted the Baikal region's air and water.

My car had many parts—pistons, wheels, the transmission—made at least partially of aluminum by dozens of subcontractors in

A Brief History of the Car

1877	Nikolaus Otto of Germany invents internal combustion engine.
1886	Karl Benz of Germany invents first practical automobile.
1903	First U.S. speed traps set to catch drivers exceeding 20 miles per hour.
1905	First car theft reported in St. Louis, Missouri.
1908	Henry Ford's Model T, world's first mass-produced car, introduced. Seats kept short to discourage romantic trysts.
1921	First drive-in restaurant—Royce Hailey's Pig Stand in Dallas, Texas—opens.
1940	Pennsylvania Turnpike, America's first "superhighway," opens.
1955	First McDonald's opens in suburban Chicago.
1956	President Dwight Eisenhower signs Interstate Highway Act. First indoor shopping mall opens near Minneapolis.
Late 1960s	Nearly 40 percent of U.S. marriages reportedly proposed in cars.
1995	United Nations scientific panel announces that human activity has begun to alter planetary climate; motor vehicles and other fossil-fuel burners primarily responsible.

Asia and America. The 125 pounds of unrecycled aluminum began as 625 pounds of bauxite mined in Australia, Guinea, and
Jamaica and smelted with hydropower from dammed rivers in
Washington, Tennessee, Quebec, and Russia. One car wheel alone
contained more aluminum than the entire bicycle.

Synthetics My bicycle had nylon cable guides made in Delaware; polyurethane handlebar grips made in Italy; a vinyl and polyurethane seat; and knobby, mud-splattered tires of butadiene rubber from Taiwan—in all, about eight pounds of synthetic materials.

After the car body was painted, unionized autoworkers earning $16 an hour installed "hard trim" such as windshields, win-
dows, and mirrors (90 pounds of glass made in Pittsburgh and
Nashville). Then they glued and snapped in "soft trim." This included the instrument panel (PVC made in Delaware and electronics from Japan), door pads (polypropylene from New Jersey),
seats (steel, foam, and vinyl from Illinois), and carpets (sewn in
Georgia of nylon and rayon from various chemical plants). Each
year, U.S. auto manufacturers consume 683 million pounds of petrochemical glues and adhesives plus 135 square miles of carpet,
enough to cover the city of Detroit.

Rubber Probably the biggest use of synthetic chemicals in my car
was in the tires. They were manufactured in Alabama of steel wires;
rayon fabric synthesized from Arkansas pine pulp; and rubber made
from Mexico petroleum, Louisiana sulfur, and various additives.

My car contained 136 pounds of synthetic rubber, the bicycle
about 5. Some 70 percent of synthetic rubber produced worldwide becomes car tires and other auto parts. Landfills, vacant lots,
and ravines in the United States hold about 2 billion old car tires.
That's eight for me and eight for every other person in the country. More than 200 million tires are added to the pile each year.

My bike and my car rolled off their respective assembly lines and were trucked to the Seattle area. Nine cars fit on the truck from Detroit; 500 bikes in cardboard boxes fit on the truck from Wisconsin. The boxes would later be recycled, thrown out, or re-used by University of Washington students shipping their bikes home at the end of the school year.

What to Do?!

- If you have a car, drive it as little as possible.

    One way to minimize your driving is to have a car that doesn't run particularly well. If it's a joy to drive the car, you'll be out there driving all the time. You want something that's unpleasant.

    —Ray Magliozzi, co-host of National Public Radio's *Car Talk*

    Combine trips, carpool, take the bus or bike, patronize nearby stores rather than far-off discount outlets, even move to a transit- and pedestrian-friendly neighborhood.
- Friends don't let friends drive sport utility vehicles. When you drive, use a fuel-efficient car.
- Shameless commercial plug: For more ideas, read *The Car and the City*. See inside back cover for ordering information.

COMPUTER

Arriving at work, I sat down at my desk and turned on my computer to check my e-mail. As I cooled off from my ride, the computer warmed up. Its screen flashed the growing number of kilobytes of memory available. But it said nothing about how many kilograms of stuff or kilowatts of energy it was using.

Electricity A 150-watt current of electricity, enough to power two incandescent light bulbs, had brought the computer to life.

The United States owns 40 percent of the world's 300 million
computers. Computers take 5 percent of the electricity used in
American offices. In comparison, lighting uses 20–25 percent.

A gun inside my monitor sent a beam of electrons across the
20-inch display, lighting colored phosphors on the inside of the
screen and a precise pattern of pixels on the outside: I had no e-
mail. The display consumed about as much power as the rest of
the computer's components combined. A "screen saver" popped
up on my screen after a few minutes, but the images of swimming
tropical fish saved no electricity: my monitor used as much power
as ever. Most of the time personal computers are turned on, they
are not actually being used. In addition, one-third of computers in
the United States are left on at night and on weekends.

Electricity in Seattle might come from anywhere on "the grid,"
the complex network of power plants and transmission lines that
keeps a constant flow of electrons available from all over the western United States and beyond. But my computer was probably
powered by a hydroelectric dam blocking a Northwest salmon
stream, and most likely of all, eastern Washington's Grand Coulee
Dam, the Northwest's largest generator of electricity. When completed in 1941, Grand Coulee walled off 1,000 miles of salmon
habitat in the upper Columbia River and exterminated North
America's largest salmon, the legendary "June hogs," chinooks more

Turn-Ons and Turn-Offs

Many people leave computers on because they believe that turning
computer equipment off and on is bad for it. In fact, turning my
computer off is *good* for it. By reducing the time it generates heat
and mechanical stress—the two leading causes of personal computer
failure—turning my computer off at night is likely to increase its
lifespan.

than five feet long and weighing 100 pounds or more. Dams have blocked more than one-third of all salmon habitat in the seven-state and one-province Columbia Basin.

Chips The beige computer that stares at me 40 hours a week consists of about 55 pounds of plastics, metals, glass, and silicon. But the heart of this fantastically intricate machine is one-fiftieth of a pound of silicon and metal formed into integrated circuits, also known as semiconductors, or simply chips.

Though the chips weigh next to nothing, making them generated more waste than making any other part of my computer. The 400-step process of making chips and covering them with millions of microscopic electrical switches began with silica mined in Washington. Silica, or silicon dioxide, the basic ingredient of sand, is the most abundant substance in the Earth's crust. The silica was heated with carbon in an Oregon plant to form carbon monoxide and 98 percent pure silicon. This silicon was heated with hydrochloric acid, then with hydrogen gas, and cooled to form a "hyperpure" silicon rod eight inches across. The crystalline

Fax à la Modem

If I used the computer's modem and my printer to read my faxes, I could have avoided buying a fax machine and the bleached, difficult-to-recycle, and annoyingly curly fax paper. If I use e-mail or print my faxes on the back sides of scrap paper, I avoid buying any new paper at all. It takes about 20 times more energy to manufacture a sheet of virgin paper than to laser-print an image onto it.

In fact, for a typical computer system, it takes at least as much energy to make a year's worth of paper as it does to run the computer for that time. Computers were supposed to herald paperless offices, but with multiple drafts and reprinting to correct every little error, computerization has probably *increased* paper—and energy—demand.

Garbage In, Garbage Out?
Waste generated in manufacturing a typical computer

Component	Product Weight (pounds)	Total Waste (pounds)	Hazardous Waste (pounds)
Chips	~0	89	7
Chip packages	1	1	0
Circuit boards	4	46	40
Monitor	50	3	2
Total	55	139	49

Does not include other computer components or waste from raw material extraction

rod was sliced into wafers less than a millimeter thick, and these were ground and chemically polished to a mirrorlike shine and trucked to the chip manufacturer in California's Silicon Valley.

The chip factory, called a wafer fab, stretched longer than two football fields and housed equipment manufactured by more than 100 companies around the world. My computer's chips—one wafer's worth—were made in "clean rooms," where only one to five particles were present in each cubic foot of air and workers wore gowns, booties, and gloves to avoid contaminating the wafers. In contrast, hospital operating rooms have 10,000 to 100,000 particles per cubic foot; outside air contains 500,000 to 1 million particles. Keeping these rooms particle free required pumping the inside air through special filters that removed fine particles. But the filters did not remove solvent vapors, some of which were toxic, from the air the workers breathed.

My silicon wafer was cleaned with acid, then heated to form a protective surface layer of silicon dioxide. Workers looking through microscopes used ultraviolet light, light-sensitive chemicals, chemical developers, patterned masks, and some of the most precise machinery ever invented to etch a pattern of minute circuits across the wafer. Further etching created holes in which high-energy machines planted phosphorus and boron, which would eventually carry electricity through my finished chips. Each of these steps was repeated several times, and after most of the steps, the chips were chemically or mechanically cleaned.

Producing the chips in my computer generated 89 pounds of waste—4,500 times the chips' own weight!—and used 2,800 gallons of water. State-of-the-art wafer fabs could have made the same chips, allowing me to do all the same computer tasks, with less than half the waste.

Paper-thin layers of Arizona copper were applied to each chip's surface, chemically etched (to create the wiring connecting the chip's circuits), cleaned, then oxidized for insulation. Machines applied an even thinner layer of gold to the back of each chip. After more chemical cleaning, a ship carried my wafer to Malaysia in a box of unbleached Oregon Douglas-fir pulp with shock-absorbing inserts of black polypropylene foam from Japan. The shippers would reuse the box and the foam inserts six times before recycling them.

Chemputer Age

About 700 different materials and chemicals went into manufacturing my computer; half of these were hazardous. Computer plant workers exposed to toxic chemicals have suffered lung diseases, skin rashes, and even increased rates of miscarriage. Electronics manufacturers have bestowed California's Silicon Valley (Santa Clara County) with large areas of contaminated groundwater and the highest concentration of Superfund hazardous waste sites in the United States.

Chemical use and pollution remain heavy in the industry, but computer manufacturers, at least in the United States, have made progress in reducing their toxic releases. According to EPA's Toxic Release Inventory, computer manufacturers generated 10 million pounds of toxic waste in 1990, two-thirds less than they did in 1987.

Chip Packages In a factory operating around the clock near Kuala Lumpur, Malaysian workers earning about $2 an hour and Japanese robots running on coal-fired electricity cut my wafer into hundreds of individual chips and assembled them into "packages." Each package consisted of a chip, frame, wires, and plastic housing. The packages enabled the chip to be wired to the rest of my computer.

Face-masked, gloved workers glued each chip to an etched copper frame, ran tiny wires of South African gold between the frame and the chip, and molded a plastic compound around the package. Because gold is so expensive, almost none is wasted. But because it is so expensive, gold miners can profitably mine ores that have less than one part per million of gold, leaving behind huge piles of mineral waste contaminated with toxic metals and the cyanide used to extract the gold.

Circuit Boards My completed chip packages were shipped back to the United States. There my computer manufacturer inserted them into printed circuit boards in the disk drives, keyboard, and other devices, as well as into the "motherboard," the main circuit board on which most internal components are mounted. I once watched a technician open up my computer to add more memory and was fascinated by the maze of boards with tiny solderlike wires zigzagging throughout like the streets of a miniature city. How unnerving, though, to rely so heavily on a piece of equipment whose workings I have little hope of understanding.

A Texas factory made my circuit boards. Their manufacture used more chemicals, energy, and water, and generated more hazardous waste, than the making of any other part of my computer. Machines cut boards made of copper, fiberglass, and epoxy resin to size, drilled holes in them, and cleaned them. In a process not unlike making chips, the holes were plated with a thin layer of copper and the boards etched with circuit patterns. This process generated airborne particulates, acid fumes, VOCs, and other chemical wastes.

Then the boards were plated with layers of copper and of tin-lead solder. The tin was imported from Brazil, and the lead was recovered from dead car batteries in Houston. Recycled lead meets 60 percent of U.S. demand annually. The United States consumes half the world's lead, mostly for car parts. Because lead is highly toxic and hard to dispose of legally, 90 percent of car batteries are recycled after use. Yet lead waste from electronic goods is almost never recycled. Scattered throughout the computer, lead solder is costly to recycle.

Etching and cleaning left behind a pattern of copper wiring on the circuit boards. Assembling and soldering the boards also produced lead, copper, VOCs, and solvent wastes.

Copper

The computer's 2.5 pounds of copper began as copper sulfide ore, much of it mined from the Chilean Andes for export to Asia. By law, 10 percent of Chile's copper revenues go to the Chilean military.

If the ore contained 0.9 percent copper (the global industry average), making my computer required excavating 280 pounds of ore and at least 300 pounds of other rock lying on top of the ore. The ore was pulverized, mixed with water and chemicals, and boiled to obtain pure copper. Boiling also produced sulfur dioxide (SO_2), which causes acid rain. Worldwide, the SO_2 emitted in copper production is equivalent to one-fourth the SO_2 emissions of all industrial nations.

Though my computer contains less copper than my car (40 pounds) or the pipes and wires in my house (even more), it was enough to have a big impact. Mining, crushing, grinding, and smelting the 2.5 pounds of copper required the energy equivalent of 73 gallons of gasoline. Mining and producing metals accounts for about 7 percent of global energy consumption.

Monitor When I use my computer, I don't see the chips, chip packages, and circuit boards hard at work on the inside. All I pay attention to is what appears on the screen—the wide end of a cathode-ray tube (CRT), a vacuum tube made of glass with electron guns at the far end. Like almost all computer monitors sold in the United States, my CRT was made in Japan.

A manufacturer in Osaka used various chemicals and ultraviolet light to etch a minute pattern of black stripes and then red, green, and blue phosphors on the glass for my monitor's front panel. Every color I see on my screen is actually a combination of these three colors.

The sides of the CRT were soldered to the front panel with lead oxide and heated, fusing the parts together to form a bulb. Discarded color monitors are classified as hazardous waste because of lead in the glass. By the year 2005, about 150 million personal computers will have been sent to landfills in the United States. They will occupy about 300 million cubic feet, equivalent to a football field stacked a mile high in computer trash.

Heart of Glass

A glassworks in Kobe made the glass for the front of my monitor, using mostly local sand and electricity from a power plant burning Australian coal. The glass also contained 5–10 percent each of strontium oxide (from Mexican ore), sodium oxide (from local salt), potassium oxide (from Russian ore), and barium oxide (from Chinese ore).

A different manufacturer made the CRT's sides. Its glass contained 22 percent lead oxide (to absorb x-rays generated by the CRT) from Australia and was coated with graphite made from Saudi petroleum. Because a monitor contains five different types of glass, and their compositions vary by manufacturer, the glass from old monitors is seldom recycled.

Ships, planes, and trucks brought the various computer components to the California plant where they were assembled. The finished computer was carefully boxed with polystyrene foam inserts and trucked to a suburban superstore. I ordered it over the phone; a delivery truck brought it to my office.

In all, the factories making my 55-pound computer generated 139 pounds of waste and used 7,300 gallons of water and 2,300 kilowatt-hours of energy (about one-fourth the energy the computer would use over its four-year lifetime). State-of-the-art factories could have made the same computer with half to two-thirds less waste. And different computers—with flat-panel displays (like those in laptop computers) instead of today's big vacuum tube monitors, for example—could have been made with even less waste.

Plastic? Tusk, Tusk

My computer was enclosed in a shell of ABS (acrylonitrile-butadiene-styrene) plastic. It was mostly Saudi Arabian oil, refined near Los Angeles. A nearby chemical plant turned the oil, along with benzene (from Wyoming coal), ammonia (from Texas natural gas), heat, catalysts, and chemicals, into the ABS ingredients. These ingredients were mixed into small pellets and injected under heat and pressure into a mold. They fused together, taking the basic shape of my computer.

Plastic has a deservedly poor environmental reputation, but it began as an environmental good guy. In 1868, during a severe shortage of tusks, a New England manufacturer of ivory billiard balls offered a $10,000 prize to anyone who could come up with a suitable replacement for ivory. A few years later, a printer from Albany, New York, won the prize with a product he called celluloid.

The world's first plastic, celluloid would later be used for (even synonymous with) motion-picture film. Yet when a British scientist had invented the substance in 1850, he deemed it useless; he gladly sold the patent rights to the American printer.

The computer industry thrives on the rapid adoption of new technologies and resists change much less than older industries. If nudged by governments and consumers, the computer industry could apply its technical expertise toward cleaning up its own act—and fast.

I stepped out to grab some lunch. I left my computer on.

What to Do?!

- Print less often. Send e-mail instead of faxes, and print on scrap paper when you can.
- Turn off your computer, or at least your screen, whenever you're not using it.
- Choose the most power-saving settings in your computer's setup. Look for EPA's Energy Star logo if you buy new equipment.
- If you need to upgrade your computer, have new memory or circuit boards added rather than replacing the whole thing.
- If you need a new computer altogether, refurbish a used one or buy a laptop, before buying a new desktop. Laptop computers weigh about one-tenth as much as desktop computers and require about one-third the electricity.

HAMBURGER

I had to eat lunch in a hurry today, so I went to a fast-food joint. I ordered a cheeseburger—hold the pickles.

Beef The quarter-pound patty of "USDA Choice" beef probably came from a steer that grazed for the first year of its life on private lands in the midwestern United States. But it's possible that the steer grazed on public lands in the West. There, cattle have left about 10 percent of arid lands desertified—barren—and about

two-thirds substantially degraded. Streamside habitats, cornerstones
of arid landscapes, have especially suffered.

At one year of age, the steer rode a cattle car to a feedlot in
Colorado. There, it spent six months eating corn plus some soybean meal, sorghum, and barley.

Grain In the feedlot, workers driving heavy machinery spread
the feed mixture in troughs as long as city blocks. The steer nuzzled
into a trough and ate. Every 1.2 pounds of feed it ate turned into
another quarter-pound patty of muscle tissue. Feedlots and other
animal raisers feed more than 70 percent of the U.S. grain harvest
to livestock each year; the largest share goes to cattle. U.S. livestock
eat 60 percent of the nation's corn harvest, or about one-fourth of
all corn grown in the world.

The pound of corn required to make my quarter-pound burger
grew on six square feet of former prairie in Nebraska. Monoculture fields have replaced virtually all native grasslands on the American plains, which may be why I remember being so bored when I
drove across them a few years ago: it all seemed the same. The
cornfield, owned by a distant corporation and managed by local
contractors, was sprayed with fertilizers, irrigation water, and pesticides including atrazine. Atrazine is the most heavily applied pesticide in U.S. agriculture; it was the second most commonly de-
tected pesticide in a national survey of drinking-water wells. If
ingested, atrazine promotes the formation of hormones that have
been linked with breast cancer. Like 40 percent of all pesticides
applied in the United States, atrazine mimics hormones in our
bodies. Among other effects, hormone mimics can cause reproductive disorders in adults and interfere with fetal development.

To produce the quarter-pound hamburger required as much
energy as one cup of gasoline would provide. Some of the energy
was used in the feedlot or in transportation, but most of it went to

fertilizing the feed. Nitrogen fertilizer is essentially congealed natural gas: a Texas chemical plant heated methane from natural gas to form hydrogen gas, compressed and superheated the hydrogen, added nitrogen distilled from air, and ended up with ammonia. The U.S. economy consumes nearly a pound of ammonia per person per day, mostly as fertilizer.

Moist and Juicy
Water consumed to make a quarter-pound hamburger in California

Ingredient	Gallons
Beef (4 oz.)	616
Cheese (1 oz.)	56
Bun (2 oz.)	25
Ketchup (1 oz.)	3.2
Tomato (1 oz.)	1.8
Lettuce (1 oz.)	1.3

The ammonia was oxidized and then combined with more ammonia to form ammonium nitrate, the key ingredient of nitrogen fertilizer. (Ammonium nitrate is also an ingredient in explosives.) Finally, the factory formed the nitrate solution into pellets, which contractors injected into the soil of the Nebraska cornfield. Small amounts percolated into streams and groundwater supplies. In rivers and lakes, excess nitrogen causes algal blooms, which can suffocate fish and other aquatic life. One-fourth of all U.S. fertilizer is applied to corn eaten by livestock.

Producing the hamburger patty required more than 600 gallons of water. Because rainfall was low and unreliable, center-pivot sprayers (the kind that make the giant green circles I've seen when flying across the country) pumped irrigation water from underground aquifers. Forty percent of U.S. beef cattle are fattened by mining ancient water from the dwindling Ogallala Aquifer of Colorado, Kansas, Nebraska, and Texas.

By eating the quarter-pound hamburger, I also caused the loss of five times the patty's weight in topsoil. Half of U.S. cropland is planted with hay, grains, and other crops to feed livestock. Hay is a soil-conserving groundcover, but row crops such as corn and soybeans are not. They leave the soil exposed and susceptible to erosion by wind and rain.

Wastes My burger caused emissions of the greenhouse gases methane and carbon dioxide. The methane came both from the steer's flatulence and from manure as it decomposed in a feedlot sewage lagoon. The carbon dioxide came from the fossil fuels used to make fertilizers and to power the farm and feedlot. The greenhouse gases emitted in producing my burger were equivalent to those emitted in my six-mile commute by car. The manure lagoon also leaked nitrogen into nearby streams and groundwater.

The steer, once fattened to Choice grade, was slaughtered. A packing plant ground, portioned, and froze the burger patty between two squares of waxed paper inside a plastic-lined cardboard box. A tractor trailer hauled it to the Northwest. It went from the distributor's warehouse to the fast-food outlet near my office, where a teenaged cook (earning $5 an hour) fried it for me on a stainless-steel grill.

Condiments The cook slapped an orange square of cheese on my burger. The cheese came from dairy herds on the Oregon coast. Manure from these herds raises bacteria concentrations in some coastal waters to unsafe levels. Sometimes, when I hike on the coast, I see the signs warning against eating shellfish. Next time I'll wonder if my cheeseburger was partly to blame.

Ketchup

Ketchup is descended from the tangy Chinese sauce ke-tsiap; in Malaysia and Indonesia today, kechap is the word for soy sauce. British sailors found Malay locals using kechap and brought it back to England in the early 1700s. Chefs tried to duplicate it but substituted mushrooms, walnuts, and cucumbers for the tropical ingredients they lacked. Not until the 1790s were tomatoes used in ketchup. Before then, most Europeans believed the tomato was poisonous; the plant is a botanical relative of deadly nightshade.

The cook garnished the burger with lettuce and tomatoes from the Central Valley of California. California grows more than 40 percent of U.S. fresh produce. This produce is irrigated with federally subsidized water pumped from what were once productive salmon rivers such as the Sacramento. The typical mouthful of American food travels 1,200 miles from farm to consumer.

Bun The cook sandwiched the burger in a toasted wheat bun made in a commercial bakery at the north end of Seattle. The bakery used flour milled in Spokane. The mill used wheat grown on two square feet of soil in the Palouse region on the Idaho-Washington border. Wheat fields stretch as far as the eye can see in these rolling hills. Loose soils, rapid spring snowmelt, and extensive wheat cultivation combine to give the Palouse some of North America's worst soil erosion.

Packaging The cashier wrapped my finished hamburger in a three-ply package of paper and polyethylene and put it in a white paper sack with two paper napkins. It smelled good.

What to Do?!

Simple: Eat less beef. Almost any kind of farm-raised meat is an inefficient use of resources, but red meat (pork and beef) is most wasteful of all. Have a veggie burrito next time.

FRENCH FRIES

I ordered french fries with my burger. Not the healthiest lunch, I admit—lots of grease and salt. But it's what I was raised on, and like I said, I was in a rush.

The fries arrived, 90 of them, in a paper box. The box was made of bleached pine pulp from an Arkansas mill. My fries weighed five ounces. They were made from a single 10-ounce potato, sliced into remarkably uniform four-inch-long strips.

Potato The potato, a russet Burbank, was grown on one-half square foot of sandy soil in the upper Snake River valley of Idaho.

Ninety percent of Idaho potatoes are russet Burbanks. They were selected in the early sixties by McDonald's and other fast-food chains because they make good fries. They stay stiff after cooking.

The growing season was 150 days; my potato was watered repeatedly. Seven and a half gallons of water were applied to the potato's half-foot plot. If all of it had been applied at once, it would have submerged the soil to a depth of two feet. The water came from the Snake River, which drains a basin the size of Colorado. The Snake River valley and its downstream neighbor, the Columbia Basin, produce 80 percent of U.S. frozen french fries. Along the Snake's upper reaches, irrigators of potatoes and other crops take all the river's water. Directly below Milner Dam, west of Pocatello, the riverbed is bone-dry much of the year.

Eighty percent of the Snake's original streamside, or riparian, habitat is gone, most of it replaced by reservoirs and irrigation canals. Dams have stopped 99 percent of salmon from running up the Snake River, and sturgeon are gone from all but three stretches. Like salmon, sturgeon migrate between fresh water and the sea, but sturgeon live up to 100 years. They do not stop growing until they die and can weigh more than 1,000 pounds. There are un-

Salt of the Earth

Sodium chloride (table salt) is one of the Earth's most common minerals. Modern miners usually inject steam underground to dissolve salt deposits. Then they pump up the brine and evaporate it to get salt.

Only 3 percent of salt ends up on food. It is much more commonly used as a de-icer and as a source of chlorine for the chemical and plastic industries. The world's largest salt eaters by far are actually cars. Every winter, road crews and property owners use 145 pounds of salt for each American—melting ice and snow from roads, parking lots, and driveways. The salty runoff heads for sewers and local streams, where it can harm aquatic life.

doubtedly sturgeon in the Snake River that remember the smell of the Pacific Ocean even though they have not been there for half a century.

My potato was treated with fertilizers and pesticides to ensure that its shape and quality were just like those of other potatoes. (My fries were so uniform that it was hard to believe they'd ever been potatoes.) These chemicals accounted for 38 percent of the farmer's expenses. Much of the fertilizer's nitrogen leached into groundwater; that, plus concentrated salts, made the water unfit even for irrigation.

Some of the fertilizers and pesticides washed into streams when rain fell. Among these were pesticides like Telone II (acutely toxic to mammals, and probably birds, through the skin or lungs) and Sevin XLR Plus (nontoxic to birds but highly toxic to fish). The Environmental Protection Agency's tests of waters in the Columbia Basin found agricultural contaminants in every tributary, including the Snake.

Processing A diesel-powered harvester dug up my potato, which was trucked to a processing plant nearby. Half the potato's weight, mostly water, was lost in processing. The remainder was potato parts, which the processing plant sold as cattle feed.

Blue Baby Syndrome

Several infants in the Tri-Cities area of southeastern Washington have developed methemoglobinemia, or "blue baby syndrome," a rare but deadly malady afflicting infants. It is caused by nitrates in drinking water. Dark-skinned babies are at higher risk because changes in their skin color can be harder to detect. Many Hispanic families work in potato fields and processing plants in the Tri-Cities area, where the Snake River joins the Columbia. Nitrates in nearly half the area's residential water wells exceed standards in the Safe Drinking Water Act.

Processing my potato created two-thirds of a gallon of waste-water. This water contained dissolved organic matter and one-third gram of nitrogen. The wastewater was sprayed on a field outside the plant. The field was unplanted at the time, and the water sank underground.

Freezing Freezing the potato slices required electrical energy, which came from a hydroelectric dam on the Snake River. Frozen foods often require 10 times more energy to produce than their fresh counterparts. In 1960, 92 percent of the potatoes Americans ate were fresh; by 1990, Americans ate more frozen potatoes, mostly french fries, than fresh ones.

My fries were frozen using hydrofluorocarbon coolants, which have replaced the chlorofluorocarbons (CFCs) that harm the ozone layer. Some coolants escaped from the plant. They rose 10 miles up, into the stratosphere, where they depleted no ozone, but they did trap heat, contributing to the greenhouse effect. A refrigerated 18-wheeler brought my fries to Seattle. They were fried in corn oil from Nebraska, sprinkled with salt mined in Louisiana, and served with ketchup made in Pittsburgh of Florida tomatoes. My ketchup came in four aluminum and plastic pouches from Ohio.

What to Do?!

- Push your elected officials to support sustainable agriculture and to stop subsidizing irrigation. The subsidies hurt the environment, taxpayers, and those who don't receive the subsidies—such as growers of rain-fed potatoes.
- Instead of buying fried, overpackaged fast food, cook some organic produce for yourself. Eat it on a real plate.
- Buy local foods or, best of all, grow your own. Garden produce is fresher, uses almost no energy except the sun, and puts to use un(der)used land—your lawn.

COLA

I dug some change out of my pocket and bought a can of cola. I saw the cola company's logo on the machine, and for the rest of the day I couldn't get that stupid jingle out of my head.

My cola was 90 percent water from the Cascades' Cedar River, carbonated at a Seattle plant. Americans drink more water carbonated in soda than they drink plain from the tap. The world drinks about 70 million gallons of soda every day.

Corn Syrup The cola contained high-fructose corn syrup from Iowa, a state where even the rain usually contains traces of pesticides. A milling plant used water, enzymes, acids, heat, grinders, and centrifuges to turn corn kernels into starch and then corn syrup. Making syrup is the second largest use of corn in North America; feeding livestock is the largest. On average, Americans consume 48 pounds of corn syrup a year.

To make my soda, the bottling plant combined corn syrup, citric acid, and flavor concentrate (a secret recipe containing flavors, preservatives, caffeine, and artificial coloring) first with water and then with carbon dioxide. The same corn-milling plant in Iowa fermented corn to make the carbon dioxide. The caffeine was a by-product of making decaffeinated coffee.

Bauxite My cola was in an aluminum can weighing 15 grams (about half an ounce). Five grams was recycled from melted-down cans and scrap. The other 10 grams began as 40 grams of bauxite ore in the Australian outback. Massive machines—with 15-foot-high tires and shovels big enough to scoop up a car—strip-mined the ore from a thin layer of underground rock. Bauxite mining destroys more surface area than mining any other ore.

Near the mine, the bauxite was crushed, washed, dried, pulverized, mixed with caustic soda from California, heated, pressurized, settled, filtered, and roasted with calcium oxide from Japan. Forty grams of bauxite yielded 20 grams of the aluminum oxide powder known as alumina, which looks like wet sugar crystals. Most of the caustic soda was captured for reuse. The process also created 16 grams of "red mud," a skin-burning mixture of oxidized metals and other contaminants. Pipes siphoned the mud to a settling pond, where a fraction of it leached into groundwater.

A Korean freighter hauled the alumina across the Pacific Ocean to the wall of breakers at the Columbia River bar, the four-mile-wide river mouth that Lewis and Clark called "that seven-shouldered horror." The ship's captain used sonar and satellite linkups to plot his course through the bar's chaotic waves and shifting sands. He motored between the two-mile-long jetties. He entered the deep channel dredged into the Columbia's shallow estuary by the Army Corps of Engineers. The dredging stirred up old sediments containing high levels of heavy metals and pesticides like DDT, which was banned 20 years ago. Jetties, dikes, and dredges have washed away or filled in two-thirds of the river's tidal marshes. Tidal marshes and other estuary habitats are nurse beds for aquatic life, sheltering young fish, birds, and many other animals.

Despite all the electronic gadgetry and all the efforts to tame the river, the bar—where the misnamed Pacific Ocean and the biggest river on the west coast of the Americas pound against each other—remained the most dangerous part of the freighter's 24-day journey. Once past the entrance, it was smooth sailing upriver toward the aluminum smelter in eastern Washington.

Smelting The smelter dissolved the aluminum oxide in giant steel pots filled with a bath of cryolite (sodium aluminum fluoride). Carbon electrodes (made from Alaskan petroleum) were low-

---

Paper-Thin Walls

The bottom of my can was arched inward; I used to think soda companies did this to give me less soda for my money. Actually, the can's walls are so thin—about a tenth of a millimeter, the thickness of a magazine cover—that the bottom has to be bowed inward. A carbonated drink pushing against a flat bottom would make the can bulge and tip over.

The pop-top side, however, cannot be arched and must be made of thicker aluminum. Most cans are tapered at the top to save aluminum: reducing the top's diameter by just 10 percent can reduce its weight by almost 20 percent. These and other improvements have made aluminum cans a third lighter than they were in 1970.

ered into the pots and delivered a massive 100,000-amp jolt of
electricity. The powerful charge broke oxygen atoms away from
the aluminum and attached them to the carbon, forming carbon
dioxide. Small amounts of fluorine attached to the carbon and
escaped the smelter in the form of perfluorocarbons (PFCs)—greenhouse gases that trap thousands of times more heat per molecule
than carbon dioxide. Few processes are as damaging to the global
climate as aluminum smelting.

Smelting is so energy intensive that aluminum earned the nick-
name "congealed electricity." Making a soda can of smelted aluminum takes energy equivalent to a quarter-can of gasoline. My
33-percent-recycled can took about a sixth of a can of gasoline of
energy.

Electricity The smelter ran on purchased hydropower 24 hours
a day. The smelter bought the electricity at discount rates from
the Bonneville Power Administration (BPA), the Pacific Northwest's
main provider of electricity. BPA markets power from 29 federal
dams and a nuclear power plant. Eight of these dams along the
main stems of the Columbia and Snake Rivers annually kill millions of young salmon heading to the Pacific. Dams, damaged stream
habitats, hatcheries, and overfishing have eliminated more than 97
percent of wild salmon in the Columbia Basin.

Aluminum smelters use almost one-fifth of the electricity sold
by BPA, yet employ very few people. The eight aluminum smelters in Oregon and Washington provide about 7,500 jobs—one-
tenth of 1 percent of the regional total. The same smelters drink
up 16 percent of all electricity used in the two states—more than
the million residents of Portland and Seattle combined. Because
BPA undercharges the smelters for electricity, other customers must
make up the difference: the average household served by BPA
pays about $2 per month extra to subsidize the smelters.

Can   The smelter's end products—giant slabs, or ingots, of aluminum—were trucked to the Seattle area. There, a mill pressed each
thick ingot into a thin rolled sheet of aluminum. Then, at another
factory, a high-powered press punched cups resembling tuna cans
out of the aluminum sheet. Other machines stretched my can out
to its final height, trimmed its edge, printed its colorful design, and
applied a clear protective varnish. Ovens baked the can twice, once
to dry the printing and once to cure a synthetic coating sprayed
on the inside of the can. At the bottling plant, machines filled the
can with near-freezing soda and immediately crimped the top on.
The can cost more than the soda inside.

I wolfed down my lunch and threw the burger wrapper, napkins, fries box, and ketchup pouch into a garbage can lined with a
polyethylene bag from Louisiana. They were later trucked to a
transfer station in Seattle's Wallingford neighborhood, where they
were packed into a 40-foot shipping container. The container was
then trucked to south Seattle and carried by rail to a landfill in
Arlington, Oregon, on the outskirts of Portland.

I threw my cola can into a recycling bin. It was one of 100
billion beverage cans used each year in the United States; 40 billion are tossed into landfills, and 60 billion are recycled. My can
was later trucked to a recycling center, shredded, and melted down.
Within two months of being tossed, it reappeared as a new can.
Recycling the can took 5 percent of the energy required to mine
and smelt a fresh one.

What to Do?!

- Buy drinks in refillable bottles, once a common form of drink
  packaging. Refillables consume much less energy than aluminum
  cans—even if 90 percent of cans are recycled. Use aluminum only
  where its light weight will save energy, as in cars or, better still, bikes.
- Drink less soda. It's just fizzy sugar water. Have some water instead.

CONCLUSION

___

"WATCH YOUR WAKE"

Thinking about all the consequences of my consumption gets me down sometimes. A friend of mine teases me about how I used to go on shopping trips but now I go on guilt trips instead. She's only kidding, but I know what she means. It's no fun to bite into some hot, salty fries and find yourself thinking about farmworkers' children with blue baby syndrome. I often resent this newfound awareness of things' secret lives. I tell myself, "If I'm some sort of global eco-villain, it's not my fault. I'm just trying to get along. It's the whole system that's cockeyed. What am I supposed to do? Stop drinking coffee? Bury my car? Join the Peace Corps?"

Confronting resource consumption is North Americans' principal environmental challenge, although few realize this fact because the impacts of consumption are mostly invisible to the consumer. The United States, with less than 5 percent of world population, consumes 24 percent of the world's energy and similar shares of other commodities (see table).

A team of researchers at the University of British Columbia recently estimated that the typical North American consumes resources each year equivalent to the renewable yield from 12 acres of farm- and forestland. For all the world's people to consume at that rate is a mathematical impossibility. It would require four Earths' worth of productive land. In other words, we're three planets short. We're at least nine planets—or atmospheres—short of safely absorbing the greenhouse gases that would result if all the world's people pumped pollution aloft at the North American rate.

To keep from getting overwhelmed, I try to focus on all the ways things are better than they used to be. My newspaper was half recycled, for example, and my fries were frozen without ozone-eating CFCs. And I focus on all the possibilities for further progress: shade-grown coffee, paperless publishing, refillable bottles.

Mostly, I try to remember that flesh-and-blood people like me preside over every step in the production, distribution, and disposal of everything I use. If all of them were constantly on the lookout for cleaner, Earth-friendly alternatives, surely I could have my coffee and read the comics without suffering through the side order of guilt. And so could everyone else.

Unfortunately, our high-consumption way of life is now the international vision of progress. The world longs to live the American dream, with steaks on the grill and two cars in the garage. Yet consumption on the North American scale—our own body weight per day—cannot last, and expanding it to all the world's people is only a fantasy. Until there is a shift toward lower resource consumption and higher quality of life here, there is little prospect of arresting ecological decline worldwide.

I can't change the world by myself, but everything I do—like biking to work today—makes a difference. Besides, I love bicycling. It gets my heart pumping and gives me a more intimate view of my neighborhood and my city.

U.S. Shares of World Consumption, 1990s

Item	Percent
Newsprint	39
Computers*	38
Plastic	33
Motor vehicles*	32
Paper	32
Aluminum	27
Copper	24
Oil	23
Beef	21
Coffee	19
Grain	16
Shoes	16
Steel	13
U.S. share of world population	**4.6**

* Share of ownership

*Broadly speaking, three factors determine how much a society con-
sumes: population, per capita consumption, and the array of technologies it uses. Environmentalists have long debated which factor
deserves the most attention, just as they have debated whether individual, corporate, or government behavior is most responsible for
our global predicament.*

*These debates, to some degree, are moot: the gap between how
our economy operates and how a sustainable economy operates is
so wide that we need progress on all fronts to achieve sustainability.
Slowing population growth is essential. So is speeding the spread of
resource-efficient technologies, from laptops to clotheslines. And so
is reducing individual consumption—through less materialistic
lifestyles as well as improvements in efficiency.*

My commute to work takes me across the old Fremont draw-
bridge over Seattle's Ship Canal. From my bike today—riding on
the sidewalk—I saw a sign down at water level that I never noticed
before from my car. It told boaters, "No Wake."

Strictly speaking, that's an impossible command. Any object
moving through water will leave some wake, no matter how small.
But as I continued my ride, I got to thinking about the idea.

*In our personal lives, we can seek to align our behavior with our
values. We can live more simply, at once reducing environmental
impacts, saving money, and leading by example. In our public lives—
in our workplaces and in our democracy—we can advocate for dramatic reforms in the systems that shape our consumption patterns.*

*We can, for example, advocate the elimination of perverse tax-
payer subsidies such as those that make aluminum too cheap and
undammed rivers too rare. And we can promote an overhaul of the
tax system. If governments taxed pollution and resource depletion,
rather than paychecks and savings, prices would help unveil the
secret lives of everyday things. Environmentally harmful goods would*

cost more and benign goods would cost less. The power of the mar-
ketplace would help propel the unstuffing of North American life.

If a boat isn't too large and doesn't move too fast, its wake won't
disturb other boats or ducks in the water, or erode the shore. Just
like boats, people—myself included—will always make waves in
the world. When you get right down to it, consumption is ines-
capable. Any biologist can tell you that life itself is a process of
consuming energy and matter and producing waste.

Yet consuming too much isn't inevitable. If there aren't too
many of us and we don't consume too fast, we won't leave any
wakes beyond the capacity of the Earth to absorb them.

The time is ripe for confronting consumption. Not only are ecologi-
cal problems like climate change more pressing than ever, consum-
erism has lost some of its allure in its North American epicenter. A
majority of Americans already feel that their quality of life is suffer-
ing because of overemphasis on work and material gain. Encroach-
ment of work and shopping on leisure time has millions of people
searching for ways to restore balance in their lives—through lifestyles
that trade money for time, commercialism for community, and things
for joy. These people—"downshifters" or practitioners of "voluntary
simplicity"—may one day attract the majority to their way of life by
demonstrating that less stuff can mean more happiness.

A North America that prospers without overusing the Earth—a
sustainable North America—is entirely possible. All the pieces of the
puzzle—from bike- and transit-friendly cities to sustainable farms
to low-impact lifestyles—exist, scattered all over the continent. All
that remains is for us to do the work of putting the pieces together.

On my way home from work, riding my bike on the opposite
sidewalk, I saw a second—and more realistic—sign along the Ship
Canal. This, I decided, was a sign worth paying attention to. It said,
"Watch Your Wake. Wish Everyone Did!"

What to Do?!

Some goods clearly have worse impacts than others. Of the items portrayed in *Stuff*, the car does by far the greatest damage on a daily basis. For most readers, reducing car use should be a top priority.

Yet ranking goods by their impacts—in effect comparing apples, oranges, and shoes—is not easy. Unraveling the life cycles of items produced in a global economy can be nearly impossible. Beyond that, some questions have no answers: which is worse, endangering Canada's salmon or polluting Taiwan's air? Remembering to choose A over B is less important than looking in a new way at the items you might buy or use. Imagine their secret lives first. With this step alone, you will probably consume less across the board.

Just as the impacts of consumption are hidden and often surprising, the solutions can be surprising as well. Using a low-flow showerhead is a good way to save water, but eating less beef— thereby saving the water used to grow cattle feed—would cut deepest of all into the 375 gallons of water consumed per person per day in the United States. Nationwide, farms use about three times as much water for irrigation as homes use for all purposes.

One of the best ways to reduce material consumption is to focus on the nonmaterial things often lacking in our lives. We sometimes consume for lack of something better to do. Feeling lonely or dissatisfied, we shop. Lacking community, we travel. Concentrating on friendship and community may make us happier while, almost without our noticing, it trims our consumption. Is it only a coincidence that "conversation" and "conservation" are spelled with the same letters?

Appendix

This Book

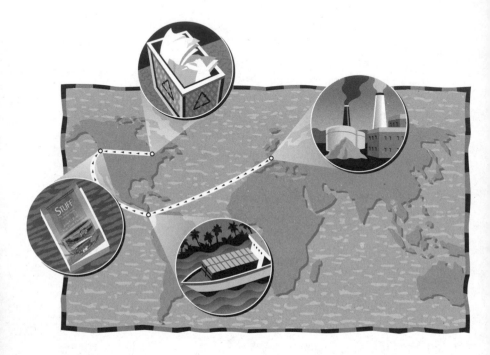

You hold in your hands an 88-page book weighing about five ounces. It is made of two types of paper, small amounts of ink and glue, and a great deal of human labor.

Text This book began with about a year's research by the authors (Alan and John) and by unpaid laborers (volunteer interns Sara, Christy, and Ankur) using telephones, computers, and published materials. Some materials were purchased or copied onto paper made from trees in various parts of North America. Some were borrowed from libraries and returned, with practically no environmental impact.

The book was written on three computers—a 60-pound desktop used by Alan, a 5.5-pound laptop used by John, and another desktop that replaced the laptop. A burglar broke into the Sightline Institute office one Sunday and stole the laptop, setting John back about a month. He hadn't backed up his files to a floppy disk in several weeks. Volunteer Peter Carlin donated his labor to find a secondhand computer (no environmental impact except for electricity use) and install an additional memory chip (for its impacts, see "Computer," page 45).

Like the athletic shoes described in its pages, the book itself was a labor-intensive product. Unlike the shoes, the book's labor cost (research, writing, editing, design, production, and distribution) far exceeded its retail price. Foundation grants and charitable contributions provided the difference.

Most drafts were read electronically or printed on the back sides of scrap paper until the outside review, editing, and design stages demanded clean paper. The office paper was made in Port Edwards, Wisconsin, along the Wisconsin River, with at least 80 percent postconsumer recycled content. Paper use in writing, editing, and designing was dwarfed by the paper used in the 9,000-copy print run.

Guts The page that your thumb is probably resting on is made entirely of postconsumer waste. The paper for the book's text—or "guts" in book-world lingo—was produced from seven ounces of old computer printouts at a mill in Saint Catharines, not far from Niagara Falls, Ontario. Three-fourths of the computer paper was collected by trucks in Ontario; one-fourth was trucked up from neighboring New York.

In the Saint Catharines mill, bales of old paper were chopped to a pulp in a water-filled tank with a giant rotating blade at the bottom—basically an oversized blender. The blender ran on electricity from a nuclear plant outside Toronto. Including the energy consumed by diesel trucks gathering curbside waste, making recycled office-grade paper (like that in your hands) uses 55 percent as much energy as making virgin paper and throwing it away. Recycled office paper also causes one-fourth the greenhouse gas emissions of virgin paper.

The pulp was piped through screens to sort out plastics and debris and then spun through a centrifuge (like the spin cycle in a washing machine) to force out dirty water. It was then lightly bleached with hydrogen peroxide synthesized from Alberta petroleum. The recycled-paper mill used almost as much water as a virgin-paper mill. The use of peroxide, rather than chlorine, meant that no dioxins were formed or released to local airs and waters. Because the paper was not de-inked during the recycling process, only 2 percent of the paper fibers were lost, and less sludge was created than with de-inking. You can see the dark flecks of ink in the paper.

Cover   Like the guts, the cover was totally chlorine free, bleached with hydrogen peroxide. Though the cover was 50 percent recycled—more than many papers being marketed as "recycled"—it had no postconsumer content (note the absence of dark flecks). We were unable to find paper made with postconsumer waste that would sharply display the cover art donated by Seattle-based artist Don Baker. (Don also happens to be the brother-in-law of Sightline Institute's Donna Morton, who supervised the book's production.)

The cover's half ounce of paper was produced in a Zanders Fine Papers mill along the Rhine River in Cologne, Germany. Half the pulp began as scraps and cuttings ("preconsumer waste") from the mill. The other half probably came from a monoculture plantation in Scandinavia or the U.S. South, but we were unable to determine its precise origin. Zanders obtained the pulp from its parent corporation, International Paper Company, the world's largest producer of pulp. International Paper has 400 facilities on four continents.

A truck carried the cover paper to the Dutch port of Rotterdam, where it was loaded on a tanker ship that would carry it through the Panama Canal and north to the printers in Vancouver, British Columbia. The guts paper was trucked west from Ontario.

The guts text is about the "greenest" of any book on the market today; the cover, however, falls short, with its lack of postconsumer content and its far too well traveled pulp: the journey from mill to printer alone spanned 14,000 miles. Overall, 93 percent of the paper used in this book was postconsumer waste; the rest came from scraps or trees. No old-growth trees went into making this book.

Printing Editor Ellen Chu mailed the book's words and pictures on computer disk to the printers in Vancouver. The printers used a laser to imprint these images on film made in Japan of PET (see "T-Shirt," page 20) and other substances. From this film and various petrochemical substances, a lithographic image was applied to plates of aluminum (smelted with hydropower in the remote coastal town of Kitimat, British Columbia). After printing, the plates would be archived for five years and then recycled.

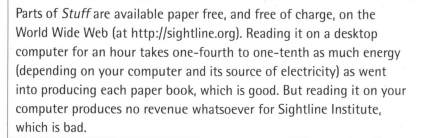

Free Stuff!

Parts of *Stuff* are available paper free, and free of charge, on the World Wide Web (at http://sightline.org). Reading it on a desktop computer for an hour takes one-fourth to one-tenth as much energy (depending on your computer and its source of electricity) as went into producing each paper book, which is good. But reading it on your computer produces no revenue whatsoever for Sightline Institute, which is bad.

The plates were then used to apply ink to poster-sized sheets of paper. The cover was printed in four colors (the standard cyan, magenta, yellow, and black). Most of the book was printed with black ink. The inks were made in Vancouver of about two-thirds soybean oil produced in Ontario; 10 percent petrochemical solvents; and the remainder, pigment. Each ink contained entirely different pigments. A manufacturer in Kentucky made the pigments, mostly from petrochemicals with depressingly long names like 2-amino-5-methylbenzenesulfonic acid. The ink was used in small amounts: one pound each of black and color inks sufficed for the entire 4,000-copy first printing.

The final step of making the book was binding it. A forklift carried stacks of printed and cut pages and covers to the bindery, located in the same Vancouver building. The guts were stacked and their inner edges cut and roughened for gluing. The synthetic glue was made in Toronto from EVA (the substance used in the midsoles of athletic shoes; see page 28) produced in Edmonton, Alberta. This glue is easily removed should the book be recycled.

Cutting the pages produced about 10 percent waste in the form of paper scraps. A truck driver picked up the scraps and drove them to suburban Burnaby, B.C., where they would be pulped and turned into cardboard boxes.

Two shipments totaling 9,000 books—110 boxes of *Stuff*—were trucked down I-5 to the Seattle offices of Sightline Institute. And, most likely, you mailed in an order form designed by Kyle Halmrast, and volunteers supervised by Rhea Connors mailed the book to you. It arrived in an unbleached envelope made along the Columbia River in Camas, Washington, of 10 percent old paper bags, 40 percent mill scraps, and 50 percent Douglas-fir trees from the Cascades. We hope you share the book with friends and reuse the envelope.

NOTES AND SOURCES

Most of the life stories told in this report are generic. They are not based on tracking specific objects back along the production line. We did not, for example, start with a particular can of cola and inquire with its distributor and manufacturer—and their suppliers and contractors—about its origins. Rather, we consulted up-to-date reports and experts about prevailing patterns in the soft drink and aluminum industries.

Thus, the stories are composite pictures, not photographs. They are reconstructions. They are based on extensive research on industry norms, production patterns, and distribution networks both globally and in the Northwest. The goal was to tell a story that was more likely than any alternative story to be true of something consumed in Seattle, Washington. Where this high standard of evidence was unattainable, we told a story that was at least as possible as any alternative. (We did track this book's production as far back and as specifically as we could.)

We chose this composite approach in part because tracking a particular firm's product and its components is extremely difficult: companies tend not to welcome intimate examination of all their processes. This reticence is especially true for suppliers that operate far from the limelight of brand names and public relations officials. More important, though, our generic stories are more informative than brand-specific stories. Generic stories reflect the dominant trends in our economy and its interactions with the Earth. Specific stories may not reflect those trends.

UNITS
(Apology to Canadian readers)

By printing metric equivalents here, and not throughout the text, we saved two pages of paper and avoided energy use and pollution by the paper mill in Ontario. We hope you agree this was a good choice.

From	Acres	To	Hectares	Multiply by	0.4047
	Square feet		Square meters		0.0929
	Square miles		Square kilometers		2.590
	Cubic feet		Cubic meters		0.02832
	Miles per gallon		Kilometers per liter		0.4252
	Ounces		Grams		28.35
	Pounds		Kilograms		0.4536
	Short tons		Metric tons		0.9072
	Inches		Centimeters		2.540
	Feet		Meters		0.3048
	Miles		Kilometers		1.609
	Gallons		Liters		3.785
	Fahrenheit		Celsius		$(°F - 32) × 5/9$

SOURCES

Some key sources were used throughout *Stuff*. Background from A. T. Durning, *How Much Is Enough?* (New York: Norton, 1992). Commodity production, trade, population, wages, land use, crop yields, and other basic statistics from *Statistical Abstract of the United States 1995* (Washington, D.C.: U.S. Bureau of the Census, 1995) and *World Resources 1996–97* (New York: Oxford Univ. Press, 1996). Average ore grades from J. E. Young, *Mining the Earth* (Washington, D.C.: Worldwatch Institute, 1992). Leading producers and exporters of minerals from *Mineral Commodity Summaries* (Jan. 1996) and other U.S. Geological Survey (USGS) documents on USGS World Wide Web site (http://minerals.er.usgs.gov).

Per capita solid waste generation from U.S. Environmental Protection Agency (EPA), *Characterization of Municipal Solid Waste in the United States: 1994 Update* (Washington, D.C.: 1994). Per capita consumption figures for coal, oil, and gas are for 1993; others for 1994, from sources above and Aluminum Association, "Aluminum—Know the Facts," Washington, D.C., July 1996. Wood estimate based on R. W. Haynes et al., *The 1993 RPA Timber Assessment Update* (Ft. Collins, Colo.: U.S. Forest Service, 1995), assuming an average density of 56 pounds per cubic foot of fresh-cut wood.

Coffee Main sources: R. A. Rice and J. R. Ward, *Coffee, Conservation, and Commerce in the Western Hemisphere* (Washington, D.C.: Smithsonian Migratory Bird Center [SMBC] and Natural Resources Defense Council, 1996); N. J. H.

Smith et al., *Tropical Forests and Their Crops* (Ithaca, N.Y.: Cornell Univ. Press, 1992); W. Roseberry, "To the Last Drop," *Report on the Americas,* Sept. 1991. Colombia's biological diversity and average pesticide use per hectare from *World Resources 1992–93* (New York: Oxford Univ. Press, 1992). Wages from Mark Schapiro, "Muddy Waters," *Utne Reader,* Nov.–Dec. 1994. U.S. consumption and numbers of beans per cup and per tree provided by Ted Lingle, Specialty Coffee Association, Long Beach, Calif., private communication, Oct. 1, 1996. Trade figures from "Why Migratory Birds Are Crazy for Coffee," SMBC, Fact Sheet No. 1, Washington, D.C., 1994.

Everglades from E. Culotta, "Bringing Back the Everglades," *Science,* June 23, 1995; J. P. Cohn, "Restoring the Everglades," *BioScience,* Oct. 1994. Sewage process from S. McGrath, "Be Careful What You Flush: It May Clog the Waters," *Seattle Times,* Jan. 28, 1996.

Newspaper Newsprint primarily from *B.C.'s Pulp Mills: Effluent Status Report* (Victoria: B.C. Ministry of Environment, Lands, and Parks, 1994); R. Kroesa, *Greenpeace Guide to Paper* (Vancouver, B.C.: Greenpeace Books, 1990); and several articles in *Reiterate* (newsletter of the Recycling Council of British Columbia), Vancouver, Jan. 1993. Advertising's share of newspaper from Andrew Sullivan, "Buying and Nothingness," *New Republic,* May 8, 1989. Newsprint production numbers from B.C. Stats, Victoria, Nov. 26, 1996, and U.N. Food and Agriculture Organization, *Yearbook of Forest Products* (Rome: 1995).

Logging employment from J. C. Ryan, "Northwest Employment Depends Less on Timber and Mining," *NEW Indicators* series, Nov. 1994; wages from Statistics Canada, Vancouver, Oct. 22, 1996. Logging's impacts from L. E. Harding and E. McCullum, eds., *Biodiversity in British Columbia: Our Changing Environment* (Vancouver: Canadian Wildlife Service, 1994); Merran Smith, Sierra Club of British Columbia, Victoria, private communication, Oct. 8, 1996; and Paul George, Western Canada Wilderness Committee, Vancouver, private communication, Sept. 9, 1994.

Salmon numbers from T. G. Northcote and D.Y. Atagi, "Pacific Salmon Abundance Trends in the Fraser River Watershed Compared with Other British Columbia Systems," paper presented at "Pacific Salmon and Their Ecosystems: Status and Future Options," Seattle, Jan. 10–12, 1994.

Logging roads from J. C. Ryan, "Roads Take Toll on Salmon, Grizzlies, Taxpayers," *NEW Indicators* series, Dec. 1995. CO_2 emissions from B.C. old-growth logging from J. C. Ryan, "Greenhouse Gas Emissions on the Rise in the Northwest," *NEW Indicators* series, Aug. 1995.

Energy requirements and pollution levels from R. Kroesa, *Greenpeace Guide to Paper,* and *Paper Task Force Recommendations for Purchasing and Using Environmentally Preferable Paper* (New York: Environmental Defense Fund, 1995). Average household refrigerator in the U.S. uses 172 watts, from A. T. Durning, "Setting Our Houses in Order," *World Watch,* May/June 1988. Numbers of recycled newspapers from Newspaper Association of America Web site (http://www.naa.org), Nov. 1996. Inks from Mimi McLeod, Seattle Times, Seattle, and Chris Knipp, US Inks, Tukwila, Wash., private communications, Sept. 20, 1996.

T-Shirt Based largely on Franklin Associates, "Resource and Environmental Profile Analysis of a Manufactured Apparel Product," prepared for the American Fiber Manufacturers Association, Washington, D.C., June 1993; J. A. H. Walsh and M. S. Brown, "Pricing Environmental Impacts: A Tale of Two T-shirts," *Illahee*, fall–winter 1995; C. M. Benbrook, *Pest Management at the Crossroads* (Yonkers, N.Y.: Consumers Union, 1996); and private communications with industry experts who asked not to be identified.

Drilling and refining from "Oil and Gas," *Standard & Poor's Industry Surveys*, Mar. 28, 1996, and EPA, *Profile of the Petroleum Refining Industry* (Washington, D.C.: 1995). PET manufacturing process from *Kirk-Othmer Encyclopedia of Chemical Technology*, 3rd ed. (New York: Wiley, 1980), and *Encyclopedia Americana*, international ed. (Danbury, Conn.: Grolier, 1994). U.S. plastic production from "Synthetic Chemicals," *Standard & Poor's Industry Surveys*, Jan. 19, 1995.

Cotton's share of world pesticide use and organic acreage from "Cotton, Pesticides and Organic Cotton" (fact sheet), Pesticide Action Network, San Francisco, June 1996. Rate of dye waste from P. Schneider, "The Cotton Brief," *New York Times*, June 20, 1993. Reproductive effects from T. Colborn et al., *Our Stolen Future* (New York: Penguin Books, 1996). Crop dusting from "Appendix F: Cotton Production," in Council on Economic Priorities (CEP), *Nike: A Report on the Company's Environmental Policies and Practices* (New York: 1993).

Irrigation from U.S. Bureau of the Census, *1987 Census of Agriculture*, vol. 3, part 1 (Washington, D.C.: U.S. Government Printing Office [GPO], 1990). Hazardous properties of textile dyes from Charles Austin, industrial hygienist, Amalgamated Clothing and Textile Workers Union, New York, private communication, Feb. 24, 1992. Honduran wages from N. Gibbs, "Cause Celeb," *Time*, June 17, 1996. Sunlight from *Energy Ideas*, newsletter of the Center for Study of Responsive Law, Washington, D.C., spring–summer 1996.

Shoes This section follows a name-brand product—a pair of Nike shoes— rather than an anonymous "typical" pair. But Nikes are the biggest-selling athletic shoes in the world, sold by the world's largest shoe company. More information is available about Nike than other companies for two reasons. Because Nike's labor practices have been criticized, many journalists have written about conditions inside Nike plants. And because Nike promotes its environmental efforts, it has provided more information about its manufacturing processes than other companies have. "Suraya" is a fact-based fictional character.

L. A. Gear quote and other information from D. Katz, *Just Do It: The Nike Spirit in the Corporate World* (New York: Random House, 1994). Shoe ownership from A. Cantwell, "Intermodal Links Speed Shipments to Market," *Journal of Commerce,* May 3, 1993. Children's-shoe spending from R. Young, *Sneakers: The Shoes We Choose* (Minneapolis: Dillon Press, 1991).

Korean labor from P. M. Rosenzweig, "International Sourcing in Athletic Footwear: Nike and Reebok," Harvard Business School, Cambridge, Mass., July 1994. Leather tanning from CEP, *Nike: A Report on the Company's Environmental Policies and Practices;* "Leather," *Encarta* CD-ROM (Redmond, Wash.: Microsoft and Funk & Wagnall's, 1994); G. Taylor, "U.S. Hide Exports Sustain Asian Footwear Producers," *Journal of Commerce,* May 2, 1994; and D. Harper, "Production of Footwear Is Truly International," *Journal of Commerce,* May 3, 1993. Korean water contamination from "Rapidly Industrializing Countries: Forging New Models," in *World Resources 1992–93.*

International shipping from I. Putzger, "Lower Rates into U.S. May Lure More Shippers," *Journal of Commerce,* May 6, 1996; P. Tirschwell, "Ship Lines Slash Rates from Asia," *Journal of Commerce,* May 6, 1996; and D. Harper, "Classification Rules Are No Walk in the Park for Shoe Importers," *Journal of Commerce,* May 1, 1995.

Synthetic materials and properties from K. E. Easterling, *Advanced Materials for Sports Equipment* (London: Chapman & Hall, 1993). Synthetics' share of rubber from "Rubber," *Encarta* CD-ROM. Waste from Nike Environmental Action Team, "Nike Regrind," Beaverton, Ore., 1995.

Factory conditions and processes from N. Baker, "The Hidden Hand of Nike," *Oregonian,* Aug. 9, 1992; M. Clifford, "Pain in Pusan" and "Spring in Their Step," *Far Eastern Economic Review,* Nov. 5, 1992; "On the Fast Track," *Indonesian Business Weekly,* Feb. 26, 1993; and various issues of *Nike in Indonesia,* newsletter of Press for Change, Bayonne, N.J., 1995–1996. Rahmad quote from J. Shakespeare, "Nike Work at 16p an Hour? Just Do It," *London Observer,* Dec. 3, 1995. Wage from E. A. Gargan, "An Indonesian Asset Is Also a Liability," *New York Times,* Mar. 16, 1996.

Shoe boxes from Rick Hastings, Nike, speech at Association of Oregon Recyclers (AOR) Annual Meeting, Seaside, Ore., Sept. 7, 1996.

Bike (and Car) Bicycle analysis based on M. D. Lowe, *The Bicycle: Vehicle for a Small Planet* (Washington, D.C.: Worldwatch Institute, 1989); A. Erlbach, *Bicycles* (Minneapolis: Lerner, 1994); Bridgestone Cycle (USA), *The 1994 Bicycle Catalogue from Bridgestone* (San Leandro, Calif.: 1994); Sheldon Brown, Harris Cyclery, Boston, private communication, Aug. 7, 1996; Grant Petersen, Rivendell Bicycle Works, Walnut Creek, Calif., private communication, Aug. 11, 1996. Bicycle's superlative efficiency from *The New Illustrated Science and Invention* (Westport, Conn.: H. S. Stuttman, 1989).

Car analysis assumes a car getting 25 miles per gallon, after U.S. Congress, Office of Technology Assessment, *Saving Energy in U.S. Transportation* (Washington, D.C.: GPO, 1994), and composed of materials as listed in American Automobile Manufacturers Association (AAMA), *Motor Vehicles Facts & Figures*

95 (Detroit: 1995). It relies heavily on EPA, *Profile of the Motor Vehicle Assembly Industry: EPA Office of Compliance Sector Notebook Project* (Washington, D.C.: GPO, 1995) and on Motor Vehicle Manufacturers Association (MVMA), *Making the Car* (Detroit: 1992).

Miles driven, Magliozzi quote, and various pollution impacts from S. Nadis and J. J. MacKenzie, *Car Trouble* (Boston: Beacon Press, 1993). Transportation costs from Puget Sound Regional Council, Transportation Pricing Task Force, "The Costs of Transportation," Seattle, Oct. 1996. Pollution per commute based on U.S. Dept. of Transportation, Federal Highway Administration, *The Environmental Benefits of Bicycling and Walking* (Washington, D.C.: 1993). Accidents from National Safety Council, *Accident Facts, 1995* (Itasca, Ill.: 1995) and J. M. McGinnis and W. H. Foege, "Actual Causes of Death in the United States," *Journal of the American Medical Association,* Nov. 10, 1993.

Space requirements from M. D. Lowe, *Alternatives to the Automobile: Transport for Livable Cities* (Washington, D.C.: Worldwatch Institute, 1990). People per hour from Lowe, *The Bicycle.* Road mileage from J. C. Ryan, "Roads Take Toll." Car fluids from Todd Litman, *Transportation Cost Analysis* (Victoria, B.C.: Victoria Transport Policy Institute, 1995).

Steel manufacturing from EPA, *Profile of the Iron and Steel Industry: EPA Office of Compliance Sector Notebook Project* (Washington, D.C.: GPO, 1995) and "Steel: Process and Toll," in *The 1994 Bicycle Catalogue from Bridgestone.* Energy savings and recycled steel content from Steel Recycling Institute brochures, Pittsburgh, Pa., 1996. Cars' carbon monoxide emissions from EPA Office of Policy, Plannning and Evaluation, *Inventory of U.S. Greenhouse Gas Emissions and Sinks: 1990–1993* (Washington, D.C.: 1994). Water use from EPA, Office of Water, *Liquid Assets: A Summertime Perspective on the Importance of Clean Water to the Nation's Economy* (Washington, D.C.: 1996). Mining's toxic waste from "An Off-the-Books Polluter," *High Country News,* Sept. 16, 1996.

Paint from EPA, *Profile of the Motor Vehicle Assembly Industry; Kirk-Othmer Encyclopedia of Chemical Technology,* 4th ed. (New York: Wiley, 1993); and Janice Camp, Univ. of Washington, Dept. of Environmental Health, Seattle, private communication, Nov. 21, 1996.

Aluminum from J. S. Gitlitz, "The Relationship Between Primary Aluminum Production and the Damming of World Rivers," International Rivers Network, Berkeley, Calif., Aug. 1993, and P. Plunkert, "Aluminum," Statistical Compendium, no date, on USGS Web site (http://minerals.er.usgs.gov).

Sightline Institute's estimate that it takes 13 percent as much energy to make a typical car as the car consumes in gasoline over its lifetime based mainly on mining figures from W. Berends et al., *While Stocks Last: A Case for Sustainable Resource Management* (Amsterdam: Friends of the Earth Netherlands, 1996) and on General Motors Corporation, *Environmental Report* (Detroit: 1995).

Glues and carpet from A. J. Darnay, ed., *Manufacturing USA,* 3rd ed., vol. 2 (Detroit: Gale Research, 1993). Tires from EPA, *Profile of the Rubber and Plastics*

Industry: EPA Office of Compliance Sector Notebook Project (Washington, D.C.: GPO, 1995) and *The New Illustrated Science and Invention*. Rubber from "Synthetic Chemicals," *Standard & Poor's Industry Surveys,* Jan. 19, 1995. Car history based on Nadis and MacKenzie, *Car Trouble,* and D. Yergin, *The Prize: The Epic Quest for Oil, Money, and Power* (New York: Touchstone, 1991).

Computer Based primarily on Microelectronics and Computer Technology Corporation (MCC), *Environmental Consciousness: A Strategic Competitiveness Issue for the Electronics and Computer Industry—Comprehensive Report: Analysis and Synthesis, Task Force Reports and Appendices* (Austin, Tex.: 1993), which analyzes the impacts of the main components of a typical workstation, and on EPA, *Profile of the Electronics and Computer Industry: EPA Office of Compliance Sector Notebook Project* (Washington, D.C.: GPO, 1995). Energy, water, and waste figures, from MCC report, exclude raw material extraction.

Benefits of turning off computer from EPA, Air and Radiation, "Purchasing an Energy Star Computer," Washington, D.C., Jan. 1995. Lighting's energy consumption from Jesse Saxon, EPA, Energy Star Programs, private communication, Oct. 17, 1996. Paper's energy consumption from S. P. Rhodes, Scientific Certification Systems, Oakland, Calif., "An Analysis of Blue Angel Environmental Seal-of-Approval Criteria for Workstation Computers," 1995. Computer numbers from E. Juliussen and K. Petska-Juliussen, *The 7th Annual Computer Industry Almanac 1994–95* (Austin, Tex.: Computer Industry Almanac, Inc., 1994). Lost salmon habitat from Northwest Power Planning Council, *Strategy for Salmon,* vol. 1 (Portland: 1992); Grand Coulee from William Dietrich, *Northwest Passage: The Great Columbia River* (New York: Simon and Schuster, 1995).

Silicon Valley contamination from Ted Smith and Phil Woodward, *The Legacy of High Tech Development* (San Jose: Silicon Valley Toxics Coalition et al., 1992). Lead from W. Woodbury, "Lead," Statistical Compendium, no date, on USGS Web site. Lead recycling from MCC, *Environmental Consciousness.* Shipping box reuse from Dave Heasty, Intel, Hillsboro, Ore., speech at AOR Annual Meeting, Sept. 7, 1996.

Fiberglass from *Kirk-Othmer Encyclopedia of Chemical Technology,* 4th ed. Plastic from EPA, *Profile of the Organic Chemicals Industry: EPA Office of Compliance Sector Notebook Project* (Washington, D.C.: GPO, 1995) and EPA, *Profile of the Rubber and Plastics Industry.* Trash from Carnegie Mellon University (CMU), *Design Issues in Waste Management* (Pittsburgh: CMU Dept. of Social and Decision Sciences, 1991).

Copper impacts based on Berends et al., *While Stocks Last,* and on Young, *Mining the Earth.* Waste rock in open-pit copper mining from R. B. Gordon et al., *Toward a New Iron Age? Quantitative Modeling of Resource Exhaustion* (Cambridge, Mass.: Harvard Univ. Press, 1987). Plastic's origins from Charles Panati, *Panati's Extraordinary Origins of Everyday Things* (New York: Harper and Row, 1987).

Hamburger Relies heavily on A. Durning and H. Brough, *Taking Stock:Animal Farming and the Environment* (Washington, D.C.:Worldwatch Institute, 1991), and A. Durning, "Fat of the Land," *World Watch,* May/June 1991. Grazing and desertification from U.S. Dept. of the Interior, Bureau of Land Management, "State of the Public Rangelands 1990:The Range of OurVision,"Washington, D.C., 1990. Pesticides in rain from "Vital Signs," *World Watch,* Sept./Oct. 1992.

Grain per hamburger from Cattle-Fax, Inc., "Grain Utilization in the Livestock and Poultry Industries," Englewood, Colo., Dec. 8, 1989. Share of grain used for feed from USDA, Foreign Agricultural Service, "World Cereals Used for Feed" (unpublished printout),Washington, D.C., Apr. 1991. Livestock's share of corn from *Encarta* CD-ROM. Atrazine use and effects from C. Cox, "Pesticides and Breast Cancer: Prevention Is Crucial," and "Currently Used Pesticides Linked with Breast Cancer," both in *Journal of Pesticide Reform,* spring 1996, and Benbrook, *Pest Management at the Crossroads.*

Energy use per hamburger from D. Pimentel et al., "The Potential for Grass-Fed Livestock: Resource Constraints," *Science,* Feb. 22, 1980. Fertilizer from *Kirk-Othmer Encyclopedia of ChemicalTechnology,* 3rd ed.; *Encyclopedia Americana;* and *The New Illustrated Science and Invention.*

Water use from M. Kreith, "Water Inputs in California Food Production," Water Education Foundation, Sacramento, Sept. 1991. Share of beef from Ogallala zone from J. B.Weeks et al., *Summary of the High Plains Regional Aquifer-System Analysis* (Washington, D.C.: GPO, 1988). Manure nitrogen from G. R. Hallberg, "Nitrate in GroundWater in the United States," in R. F. Follett, ed., *Nitrogen Management and GroundWater Protection* (Amsterdam: Elsevier, 1989).

California's share of produce from J. Hollender, *How to Make the World a Better Place* (NewYork:William Morrow, 1990). Food travel from U.S. Dept. of Defense, *U.S. Agriculture: Potential Vulnerabilities,* cited in Cornucopia Project, *Empty Breadbasket?* (Emmaus, Pa.: Rodale Press, 1981). Ketchup from Panati, *Panati's Extraordinary Origins of Everyday Things.*

French Fries Based largely on W. Bean and D. Runsten, *Value Added and Subtracted: The Processed Potato Industry in the Mid-Columbia Basin* (Portland, Ore.: Columbia Basin Institute, 1993), and on T. Palmer, *The Snake River* (Washington, D.C.: Island Press, 1991). Also based on Gary Lucier, potato specialist, USDA, Economic Research Service, Washington, D.C., private communication, Nov. 22, 1996; EPA, Region 10 Office, *Columbia River Basin Water Quality Summary Report* (Seattle,Wash.: 1992); E. P. Jorgensen, ed., *The Poisoned Well* (Washington, D.C.: Island Press, 1989); and P. Koberstein, "Blue Babies, Hot Potatoes," *Cascadia Times,* Aug. 1996.

Pesticide toxicities from "Pesticides Approved for Use on Klamath Basin Refuges in 1996 [box]," *Cascadia Times,* Aug. 1996. Energy consumption from D. Pimentel, "Energy Flow in the Food System," in D. Pimentel and C.W. Hall, eds., *Food and Energy Resources* (Orlando, Fla.: Academic Press, 1984). Coolants

from H. French and E. Ayres, "A Refrigerator Revolution," *World Watch*, Sept./
Oct. 1996. Salt from M. Visser, *Much Depends on Dinner* (New York: Collier,
1986), and "Sales by Major End Uses," Salt Institute Web site (http://
www.saltinstitute.org), Sept. 1996.

Cola Cola and corn syrup from A. Durning, "Junk Food, Food Junk," *World
Watch*, Sept./Oct. 1991; cola-making process and global consumption from A.
Erlbach, *Soda Pop: How It's Made* (Minneapolis: Lerner, 1995).

Recycling provides one-third of U.S. aluminum according to Aluminum
Association, "Aluminum—Know the Facts." Mining and smelting from Young,
Mining the Earth; J. E. Young, "Aluminum's Real Tab," *World Watch*, Mar./Apr.
1992; and "Aluminum: Process and Toll," in *The 1994 Bicycle Catalogue from
Bridgestone.*

Columbia River bar description from T. Egan, *The Good Rain: Across Time
and Terrain in the Pacific Northwest* (New York: Vintage, 1991). Tidal marsh losses
from A. E. Copping and B. C. Bryant, *Pacific Northwest Regional Marine Research
Program,* vol. 1 (Seattle: Univ. of Washington, Office of Marine Environmental
and Resource Programs, 1993).

Smelter emissions from J. C. Ryan, "Greenhouse Gas Emissions on the
Rise in the Northwest." Wild salmon numbers based on Rich Pettit, Washington Dept. of Fish and Wildlife, Olympia, private communication, Jan. 4, 1996,
and Burnie Bohn, Oregon Dept. of Fish and Wildlife, Salem, private communication, Aug. 10, 1994. Smelter employment and electricity use from W. Th-
ompson, "Northwest Aluminum Approaches Meltdown," *Oregonian*, Feb. 6,
1994. Regional electricity use from J. C. Ryan, *Hazardous Handouts: Taxpayer
Subsidies to Environmental Degradation* (Seattle: Sightline Institute, 1995). Subsidies from Save Our Wild Salmon Coalition, *Wild Salmon Forever: A Citizens'
Strategy to Restore Northwest Salmon and Watersheds* (Seattle: 1995).

Can production and design from H. Petroski, *The Evolution of Useful Things*
(New York: Vintage Books, 1992), and Reynolds Metals Company Web site
(http://www.rmc.com/divs/can).

Conclusion: "Watch Your Wake" Twelve acres from M. Wackernagel
and W. Rees, *Our Ecological Footprint: Reducing Human Impact on the Earth*
(Gabriola Island, B.C.: New Society, 1996). Nine atmospheres based on state-
ment that 60 percent reduction in global CO_2 emissions needed to stabilize at-
mospheric concentrations at current levels from Intergovernmental Panel on
Climate Change, *IPCC First Assessment Report, Overview and Policymaker Summaries* (Geneva: World Meteorological Organization/United Nations Environment Programme, 1990); emission rates from *World Resources 1996–97.*

Consumption table based primarily on *Statistical Abstract 1995* and *World
Resources 1996–97;* Juliussen and Petska-Juliussen, *Computer Industry Almanac;*
Haynes et al., *1993 RPA Timber Assessment Update;* Ted Lingle, Specialty Cof-
fee Association, private communication; L. R. Brown et al., *Vital Signs 1993*

(Washington, D.C.: Worldwatch Institute, 1993); Aluminum Association, "Aluminum—Know the Facts"; Reynolds Metals Company Web site; P.T. Bangsberg, "China Tramples Rivals in Asia Footwear Industry," *Journal of Commerce*, May 2, 1994; and M. Carlino, "U.S. Footwear Imports Tread Flat Track in '96," *Journal of Commerce*, May 6, 1996.

American majority from *Yearning for Balance: Views of Americans on Consumption, Materialism, and the Environment* (Takoma Park, Md.: Merck Family Fund, 1995). Water from USGS, *Estimated Use of Water in the United States in 1990,* USGS Circular 1081 (Washington, D.C.: GPO, 1993).

Appendix: This Book Energy and pollution comparisons from *Paper Task Force Recommendations for Purchasing and Using Environmentally Preferable Paper.* Other information from conversations with our printers, Benwell and Atkins, Vancouver, B.C., and their suppliers: Unisource Canada, Vancouver; Flint Ink, Langley, B.C.; CDR Pigments and Dispersions, Elizabethtown, Kentucky.

John C. Ryan is research director of Sightline Institute and author of *State of the Northwest* and *Hazardous Handouts*. He has worked for local nonprofit groups in Indonesia and for Worldwatch Institute in Washington, D.C. John doesn't own a car, but he loves french fries and owns 14 pairs of shoes.

Alan Thein Durning is founder and executive director of Sightline Institute and author of books including *This Place on Earth* and *How Much Is Enough? The Consumer Society and the Future of the Earth*. He lectures widely, is a commentator on National Public Radio's *Living on Earth*, and drinks more coffee than he cares to admit.

Sightline Institute (formerly Northwest Environment Watch) is a wholly independent, not-for-profit research center based in Seattle. Its mission: To foster a sustainable economy and way of life throughout the Pacific Northwest—from southern Alaska to northern California and from the Pacific Ocean to the crest of the Rockies.